USE MY NAME:
Jack Kerouac's Forgotten Families

JIM JONES

D0802155

ECW PRESS

The publication of *Use My Name* has been generously
supported by the Government of Canada through
the Book Publishing Industry Development Program.

CANADIAN CATALOGUING IN PUBLICATION DATA

Jones, James T., 1948-
Use my name : Jack Kerouac's forgotten families
ISBN 1-55022-375-5

1. Kerouac, Jack, 1922-1969. 2. Authors, American – 20th century
– Biography. 3. Beat generation – Biography   I. Title.

PS3521.E735Z76 1998   813'.54   C98-932895-3

Front-cover photo: Jack Newsom
Imaging by ECW Type & Art, Oakville, Ontario.
Printed by AGMV l'Imprimeur, Cap-Saint-Ignace, Quebec.

Distributed in Canada by General Distribution Services,
325 Humber College Blvd., Etobicoke, Ontario M9W 7C3.

Distributed in the United States by LPC Group,
1436 West Randolph Street, Chicago, Illinois, U.S.A. 60607.

Distributed in the United Kingdom by Turnaround
Publisher Services, Unit 3, Olympia Trading Estate,
Coburg Road, Wood Green, London N2Z 6TZ.

Published by ECW PRESS,
2120 Queen Street East, Suite 200,
Toronto, Ontario M4E 1E2.

www.ecw.ca/press

PRINTED AND BOUND IN CANADA

USE MY NAME:

Jack Kerouac's
Forgotten Families

*To Tamara Goodrum, for love and
support throughout the 1990s*

A stone called asbestos is not more unquenchable than the thirst of my paternity.

— Jack Kerouac in a letter to Allen Ginsberg, July 14, 1955

The judge promised that if Jack acknowledged her, he would only have to pay $52 a month, the minimum amount of child support. Jack accepted the deal though he futilely tried to get into the record the fact that he was recognizing *her name* rather than her.

— Gerald Nicosia in *Memory Babe*

"Yes, man," he said, washing his hands at the sink, "it's a very good trick but awful on your kidneys and because you're getting a little older now every time you do this eventually years of misery in your old age, awful kidney miseries for the days when you sit in parks."

— Dean Moriarty to Sal Paradise in *On the Road*

ACKNOWLEDGMENTS

Despite the illusion that the author has created it, every book results from collaboration. In the case of the book that follows, this collaboration has been a source of great pleasure, at least for the author. I would like to acknowledge the following people, among many others, as collaborators:

For encouragement, Judith Moore, author of *Never Eat Your Heart Out*.

For information, Jan Kerouac, Paul Blake Jr., Jim Perrizo, John Sampas, Stephen Ronan, Sharon Aly, Dave Haverty, Ann Charters, Gerald Nicosia, Rod Anstee, Dan Barth.

For help, criticism, or just plain prodding: Allen Ginsberg, Eric Pervukhin, Brett Eugene Ralph, Brian Foye, Mark Hemenway, Attila Guyenis, Shari Ballard-Krishnan, Susan Little, Sallie Jo "Spike" Sorensen, Sam Lines, Anne Rearick, Diane DeRooy, Loren Reid, Robert Greiner, Maritza Jennings, Will Williams, Barbara and Dennis Radford-Kapp, Holly Potter, Jennifer Lokash, and Robert Lecker; graduate and undergraduate students at Southwest Missouri State University and elsewhere; librarians (the unsung heroes of the book business) at Southwest Missouri State University, the Missouri State Historical Library, the Bancroft Library at the University of California–Berkeley, the University of Washington, and the Seattle Public Library.

PHOTOGRAPHS

AUTHOR'S NOTE

In addition to the interviews, articles, and books cited in the text, I have relied heavily on personal correspondence and phone conversations with the people I write about in *Use My Name*. Ann Charters told me the story about her dog destroying the plants during her 1966 visit to Hyannis, and various and sundry members of the Kerouac network contributed other tidbits orally. I have freely used eight of the nine biographies of Jack Kerouac (Barry Miles's came out too recently for me to use) and *Jack Kerouac: Selected Letters, 1940–1956* to cross-check facts and to try to keep the time line straight. Following the precedent of these biographies, I have also compared fact with fiction, as presented by Jack Kerouac in *The Town and the City* and *Vanity of Duluoz*. I prepared for and supplemented my interviews with Jan Kerouac by consulting articles on her in *Moody Street Irregulars* (6/7), *Kerouac and the Beats: A Primary Sourcebook*, and *The Beats: Literary Bohemians in Postwar America*, as well as newspaper articles and reviews of her novels too numerous to mention. Jan submitted only one author's questionnaire, under the name Jan Michele Hackett, which was published in *Contemporary Authors*. In preparing the chapter on Edie Parker, I consulted bits of her memoir published in *Kerouac and the Beats* and *To William S. Burroughs* (Ridgeway Press), as well as Shari Ballard-Krishnan's 1996 master's thesis at Central Michigan University, *Frankie Edith Parker: The First Beat Woman, A Call for Recognition*. I have a draft of Joan Haverty's unpublished memoir in my possession. Two anthologies of writing by Beat women have also appeared since I began work on this book.

TABLE OF CONTENTS

O N E

THE END OF THE LINE

On the first weekend of June 1996 I found myself thumbing through the section marked "legal documents" in my black box, the portable file in which I had kept information relating to Jan Kerouac for about a year and a half, ever since I began work on a biography of the only child of America's most famous road novelist, about six months after she filed suit to gain a share of her father's estate by questioning the validity of his mother's will. Jan met Jack only twice, and when he died in 1969 at age forty-seven of the effects of alcoholism, he left everything to his mother, who survived him by just four years. After that, Jack Kerouac's estate, valued at the time at about $35,000, passed into the hands of his third wife, the former Stella Sampas. After Stella's death in 1990 her share of the royalties from Jack's novels, most of which have now come back into print, went to her surviving brothers and sisters, who elected one of their number to administer Jack's estate, now reputedly worth some $10 million. It was John Sampas, the youngest brother and administrator, who prompted my search for a copy of Jan's will by informing me of her death.

The death itself came as only a mild surprise, because Jan had suffered end-stage renal failure in the summer of 1991, and the doctors told her then she had ten years at most to live. Still, I was shocked when the event made her prognosis a reality, saddened that I had not been able to reconcile with her after our falling-out, and struck by the irony that I had to learn the news from the man Jan had come to consider her mortal enemy. The obituary in the Lowell *Sun*, Jack's hometown newspaper, said that Jan spent most of her last month alive in an Albuquerque hospital, and that doctors had removed her spleen the day before she died on

Wednesday, June 5, a painful end to a debilitating five years of semi-invalidism. I tried to remind myself that for all but those last five years, however, Jan had lived a full and carefree life, in many ways the mirror of her father's, as Dave Perry pointed out in the *Sun* obit.

I recalled my many long phone conversations with Jan during the few months of our association, when she would sometimes startle me by excusing herself to step outside to snap a photo of a particularly sumptuous New Mexico sunset, leaving me on the line to imagine her actions until she returned. Invariably, these always amusing and sometimes disturbing conversations ended with Jan's announcement, "Well, I'd better go now. It's time for my exchange." By exchange she meant her home dialysis, which she performed every six hours, come rain or come shine, by means of a peritoneal catheter implanted in her belly. I'd bid her goodnight by suggesting a topic for our next conversation, or asking if she could try to recall some forgotten detail of an event we had just discussed. More often than not, our next phone call began with her restored memory, although each memory merely served as a springboard to some other life experience. Like Jack's novels, Jan's tales often bounced around freely in time, as though the present were little more than a prompt to her memory. She was a marvelous storyteller, and like Jack, too, she was always at the center of her own tales.

Until 1990 Jan's life revolved around her eccentric mother, Joan Haverty, Jack Kerouac's second wife. As Jan frequently reiterated, her mother and she were soul mates, partners in a hard life that began for Jan on February 16, 1952, in Albany, New York. After about five years upstate, Jan went with her mother to New York City, where she grew up in haphazard fashion on the Lower East Side of the 1960s. Jan found sex early (in the form of a hundred boys she slept with, giving each one a number in sequence), drugs in great variety (she once ingested an unidentified white powder she found wrapped in tin foil lying on the sidewalk), and rock and roll only in her aspirations (she once cut a demo with two friends in hopes of making it as a girl group).

After one stay in Bellevue and another in a Bronx reformatory, aged 15 and pregnant by her drug-dealing ex-boyfriend, Jan fled to Mexico in the company of a caring young man named John Lash, now a New Age writer. It was as a prelude to that trip that she and John went to visit her father in Massachusetts. Their only previous encounter had come on the day Jack was forced to appear in court to submit to a blood test in Joan's paternity suit against him. That was 1961; this was 1967. But Jack was too far into the throes of alcoholism and too much in denial about his responsibility for his child (although he did pay support for those six years — about fifty dollars a month) to respond to Jan during her brief visit. The best he could do, when she told him she and John were going to Mexico to write a novel, was to offer his proudest asset: "Yeah, go to Mexico and write a book," he told her. "You can use my name." With this scant help she departed for the border, like any refugee, looking for a better life, hoping to start a family, and perhaps find a career. Jan's novel, an adaptation, she told me, of *The Alexandria Quartet*, never got finished. The baby was stillborn. Within six months John Lash was forced literally to carry Jan back across the border into California. Nevertheless her life on the road, as Sal Paradise says in her father's most famous novel, had begun.

By the time John Sampas called me with the news of Jan's death, my relationship with her, at first cordial and enthusiastic, then tense and acrimonious, had finally grown cold. Our falling-out occurred quickly in the days following a lengthy visit I made to Jan's house in March 1995, which I timed to coincide with the anniversary of her father's birthday, the 12th. During that week in Albuquerque Jan allowed me to peruse her files for information about her past and for legal details of her lawsuit against the Sampas family. That is how I came to have a copy of her will. I made it the day before our fateful interview about Jan's brief stint as a prostitute, the interview that precipitated her decision to dismiss me as her biographer.

I told John about the copy — one she had given me expressed permission to make. He asked if I could recall any of its details, especially whom Jan had named as executor. The copy was in my office, and I hadn't looked at it for a year. The only thing I recalled was that Jan's half-brother, David Bowers, Joan Haverty's fourth child, was the primary beneficiary of her estate. Beyond that, I couldn't say much, but I promised to fish the will out of my files and call him the next day.

John expressed his thanks in advance, as he always does when he asks a favor. "If you do this for me, Jim, I'll kiss your ass," he joked. I told him that wouldn't be necessary. Then he complained that he was tired after being on the phone all day. Before he rang off, however, I wanted to know if he would allow Jan to be buried with her grandparents and uncle, whom she had never known. "Sure, why not?" he responded. As it turned out, Jan's body was cremated, and on the first anniversary of her death, her ashes were interred next to Leo, Gabrielle, and Gerard, Jack Kerouac's parents and older brother, where they will lie together in that unlovely spot on the outskirts of Nashua, New Hampshire, for all eternity. As a footnote to this sad fact, John Sampas, who in his role as manager of the Kerouac estate had to approve the changes to the family monument, told me that the mortuary had misspelled the estranged granddaughter's name. Silently, he amended the anonymous "Jane" to read correctly.

Just a few months before her death, Jan had created a minor media splash by requesting of the cemetery board in Lowell, Massachusetts, her famous father's hometown, that his body be moved to Nashua as well, so he would rest with his parents and his saintly brother, rather than with his third wife, Stella, and her younger brother, Sebastian, Jack's first literary friend in high school. Newspaper editors responded to the news of Jan's requests with the inevitable bad puns: Kerouac's daughter wants to take her father's body on the road. Lurid things like that. A friend of mine from Lowell, faxing me the story, commented: "Is this Kerouac or Poe?" As the literary types there would be quick to point out, Poe is reputed to have stayed in the Old Worthen, the oldest tavern in a town well-stocked with both old buildings and taverns. Perhaps the master of the macabre was exercising his own kind of ironic influence on his literary descendants. And perhaps, when she complained about lacking the "psychic energy" to pursue her request after it was denied by the Lowell Cemetery Board, Jan intuited her own impending demise. Perhaps she wanted to be near her father in death, as she never was in life. In any case, irony of ironies, one of her cousins, who lives in the area, found it necessary to request permission for her burial from John Sampas, the man whom Jan had so frequently vilified, a request he granted unhesitatingly with some grace.

That night I went to my office to retrieve the will, which I read carefully. As I explained to John the next day, qualifying my statements by reminding him that fifteen months had passed since I obtained the copy, Jan might have made a new will or at

Jim Jones and John Sampas at the Sampas
family home, Lowell, MA, June 1995

least revised the old one. Nevertheless, I related the basics (which were subsequently confirmed as both accurate and current by an article in the *Los Angeles Times*) over the phone: David Bowers would share equally with Jan's first husband, John Lash, the substantial royalties from Jack Kerouac's many novels and books of poetry, most of which are currently in print, thanks to the most recent Kerouac and Beats revival — and to the marketing efforts of the Sampas family. Lash, who had met and befriended Jan when she was only fifteen, was named executor.

Then I read out an especially vicious paragraph pertinent to John: "I . . . particularly do not want any member of the Sampas family to inherit any of my estate or any part of it." I found this characteristic of Jan's antagonistic rhetoric: whenever she spoke of those who had legally inherited her father's estate, she lost all her native wit and charm. She began to sound like a hurt child, exactly as her father sounded when he thought his friends had betrayed him. The humanity of her antagonist was transformed into a demon. It seemed sad to me, who, like many people, have experienced this sort of thing in my own family. And I couldn't help thinking of something John Sampas told me when I first got to know him. He said that for years Jan's relationship with their family had been cordial, from the mid-1980s, when she first made her rightful legal claim to half the royalties from her father's books, many of which were just then coming up for copyright renewal, until 1993, when something — I myself am still not completely sure what — changed all that. But John still insists — and I believe him, though Jan's supporters would not, of course — that if she had asked, he would have given her a share of her father's estate, a share equal in value to his or his brothers' and sister's. He even claims to have invited her to come live with him in Lowell (an invitation which, from my experience, he's lucky she didn't accept). She might have got some relief that way from the ravages of the disease that killed her. She might have become, even at that late date, an honorary member of the large, intelligent, friendly clan of the Sampases.

Instead, Jan chose to file suit, though as Samuel Butler long ago observed, nothing is certain in the law but the expense. For Jan, however, the expense was minimized by a lawyer who agreed to take her case on a contingency basis, apparently in prospect of winning forty percent of a third of Jack Kerouac's $10-million estate. But she paid other costs. Some insiders, like the Beat poet Allen Ginsberg, suggested that she was killing herself by fighting an unnecessary battle, that if she would simply make peace with the Sampas family, everything would be all right (to use a phrase from Kerouac's novels). Her father's meticulously kept archive — which was moved after Jack's death to a Sampas family home on Wilder Street in Lowell, where it occupied a room of its own — would find a safe haven, where fans could come worship the sacred relics and scholars could turn them into evidence for academic arguments.

But Jan chose the road of contention, struggle, and confrontation. In this she was aided and abetted by the most thorough of Kerouac's biographers, Gerry Nicosia, a small dynamo of a man with an excellent memory for facts, a strident voice, and a penchant for self-promotion and conspiracy theories. Indeed, as at least one British journalist has intuited, Jan's battle for partial control of her father's estate also became a battle between two biographers, Nicosia and Ann Charters, the first and most popular of Kerouac's nine chroniclers, who is now favored by the Sampases for such duties as the editing of Kerouac's *Selected Letters*, the first volume of which was published about the same time Jan and I had our falling-out.

Biography is crucial to the understanding of an autobiographical novelist, whether it be Jack Kerouac or Jan Kerouac — and Jack has been the subject of no less than nine biographies in less than thirty years since his death. These two biographers, I would add, also represent regions, and part of the intellectual momentum of the dispute over Jack Kerouac's estate results from the antagonism between East and West coasts, a literary version of the question of Kerouac's final resting place: should it be the Berg Collection of the New York Public Library or UC–Berkeley's Bancroft Library's rare books division? Put in these terms, Jan's lawsuit asks, "Who will own Jack Kerouac's reputation, East or West?" Clearly, Gerry (and therefore Jan), who lives in Marin County, favors the latter, while John Sampas (and therefore Ann Charters), who still lives in the old family home on Stevens Street

Gerald Nicosia at the New York University conference on the
writings of Jack Kerouac, Washington Square Park, June 1995

in Lowell, favors the former. In fact, the Berg has been building
its Kerouac collection for many years, and some of Kerouac's
archive is already on deposit — if not display — there.

But aside from the inflated issue of whether Kerouac's papers
should all be gathered in the same location, Jan's lawsuit gave
her a reason to live. I don't for a minute believe that starting it
was her idea, however. Her mind didn't work that way. While I
was in Jan's good graces, she admitted to me that she had no
comprehension of the legal matters she had involved herself in.
She knew only what her lawyers explained to her and, I expect,
said publicly only what Gerry coached her to say. Not that Jan

was stupid. Far from it. Like her father, she was extraordinarily intelligent, with an excellent memory and a gift for languages and geography. But like most of us, her mind didn't grasp legalisms. Besides, she could barely read. When I visited her, she admitted to me that she had read only five books in the past twenty years. When I asked why, she explained that her eyesight was disturbed by a kind of constant hallucination, which she described as looking like a lace curtain. "If I focus on the curtain, I start to hallucinate, just like on LSD," she told me. Consequently, she was forced to read her correspondence through a large lighted magnifying glass mounted on a mechanical arm on her desk, to compose her third, unfinished novel, *Parrot Fever*, on tape, and to sign her name in a huge, childlike scrawl. Many observers who saw Jan perform in the few years before her death, unaware of her kidney failure or her eye problems, assumed that she was drunk or stoned, or worse yet, simply ditsy. Gerry once told me that he thought her eye condition might be something called maculation of the cornea, but Jan herself ascribed it to the aftereffects of LSD. I gather she never sought treatment for the condition, whatever its cause.

In any case, the prospect of acquiring part of her father's estate allowed her to engage in some rather outsized fantasies. One I recall from our conversations was her dream of opening a wild-animal refuge with a restaurant ("Chez Kerouac") on some Pacific island. With her $3-million settlement, Jan, a blue-water fanatic, could charter a jet to carry all her home dialysis supplies, including crates and crates of heavy, bulky sterile solution, and escape to the kind of carefree life she had lived before the onset of her disease in Puerto Rico in the summer of 1991. In other words, the lawsuit she filed in Pinellas County, Florida, where her father died, was to be her fountain of youth, her return to health and happiness, and last but not least, a recreation of her family. One of the first things she showed me when I got to her little house in Albuquerque was the "adoption papers" for a Siberian tiger, sponsored by some wildlife organization. In return for her substantial donation, Jan was given the privilege of naming the tiger: she called it Natasha, after the stillborn child she bore in the Mexican jungle in 1968. At other times, her desire to preserve her father's memory by collecting his papers in one spot took the form of a house similar to Hemingway's in Key West. But even here, Jan's desire for a permanent home for herself seemed thinly masked.

Jan also reveled in her animosity toward the Sampas family, especially John. Once she admitted to me that she regularly performed a voodoo-like ritual in which she beheaded an effigy of John Sampas on her kitchen cutting board. Of course, she may have been just pulling my leg, but even so, this fantasy, like the island paradise, is still revealing.

Jan's childishness made her charming (I have a hilarious tape of her singing a Popeye's Chicken commercial), but it also led her to make some incredibly vulgar displays of emotion. For instance, when I met with Ann Charters on the return leg of her promotional tour for *The Portable Kerouac* and *Selected Letters*, only two weeks after I had visited Jan, she told me about an encounter with Jan following a reading at Black Oak Books in Berkeley. This harassment was planned by Gerry and Jan as a prelude to a fund-raising and publicity event to be held for Jan in San Francisco. (I know, because I heard them discussing it on the speaker phone while I was staying with Jan in Albuquerque. I confessed to Ann that I felt uncomfortable about Gerry and Jan's plan to disrupt her tour. I should have called to warn her.) It was a mere coincidence that Charters' tour took her to the Bay Area just days before the planned benefit. Viking Penguin unknowingly delivered her into the hands of her enemies. Not that anyone actually threatened her, but Charters felt sufficiently intimidated that she brought a hired escort to some of her readings, and finally canceled the last one in Larkspur, near Gerry's home. After her reading in Berkeley, just a few blocks from the campus of her alma mater, Gerry tried to wrest the spotlight from her in order to present his views on the merits of Jan's lawsuit, presumably to indict Ann for complicity with the Sampas family. After a store manager restored some semblance of order and Ann was quietly signing books, Jan sidled up to her and announced crudely, "Blood is thicker than urine."

While I can't judge Jan's state of mind clinically, it seems likely that her kidney failure and subsequent hospitalization in Puerto

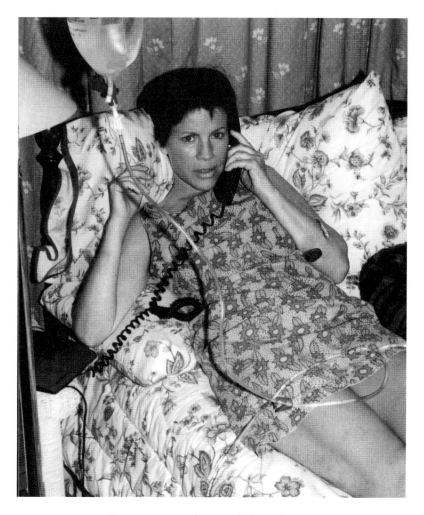

Jan Kerouac performing kidney dialysis
at home, Albuquerque, NM, March 1995

Rico and in Albuquerque made her acutely conscious not only of
her vulnerability but of her lack of family support. Jan actually
moved to Albuquerque because of the presence there of her first
husband's sister, who had been her friend since the late 1960s.
The idea for the lawsuit came just as her condition began to
stabilize — rather than go to the hospital for dialysis, Jan was able
to perform her "exchanges" at home. In 1992, after a windfall from
what Jan believed was the sale of TV rights to *On the Road*, she

fled briefly to the blue waters of Key West, and in the process of moving lost the manuscript of her first novel, *Baby Driver*. When life in the Keys, a day's bus ride from a major hospital, proved unfeasible for Jan, she returned to New Mexico, suffered a physical collapse, and nearly died. The lawsuit, whatever its origins, gave her a new reason to live, as well as the promise of a very tangible connection with her father and her father's family.

One other feature of Jan's personality figures into her attitude toward the Sampas family and explains the hostile clause in her will. That is Jan's tendency to allow herself to be manipulated by men. If you read her two published novels (*Baby Driver* and *Trainsong*), and the available excerpts from *Parrot Fever*, you quickly perceive a pattern in Jan's life: looking for both love and excitement, but clearly lacking any sense of her own worth, she continually puts herself in the hands of less than admirable men. She lets them talk her into questionable adventures, even petty crime, but when they threaten her freedom or become abusive, she abandons them in a second. The big exception to this pattern is her first husband, John Lash, who now will inherit one half of Jan's estate, and therefore half an interest in the outcome of the lawsuit.

At least in Jan's portrayal in her autobiographical fiction, John seemed to offer the balance of freedom and stability that many independent-minded people seek in long-term relationships. Why couldn't she stay with him, then? Well, probably she was simply too young to settle down. Perhaps their age difference (six years) seemed too great at the time. But perhaps John Lash was also too *unlike* Jack Kerouac. Perhaps he was just too willing to *be there* for Jan. I don't know. Lash refused to talk with me about Jan, accusing me (probably rightly) of participating in the trend of glorifying the Beats. But Jan also considered him her soul mate, and that's why despite the fact that they had been divorced for over twenty years, she left him half her money and made him executor of her will.

The lawsuit repeats the more common pattern on the legal level. Part of Allen Ginsberg's complaint about the lawsuit was that Gerry Nicosia and Tom Brill, Jan's lawyer in California, were taking advantage of a sick and vulnerable individual. There is no reason to suspect that Nicosia and Brill are dishonorable, but Gerry for his part often makes Jan look like a victim of another kind, and I don't want to downplay her willfulness in the matter of the lawsuit and her ultimate responsibility for her own actions, past and present. Remember, what brought on the kidney failure was high blood pressure probably exacerbated by drug abuse, alcoholism, and general neglect of her own health. Still, Jan describes in her autobiographical novels her own tendency to be manipulated by men with plans. It just so happens that in this case, the plan was legal.

The feature of Gerry Nicosia's public rhetoric that annoys me the most is neither his air of moral superiority nor his disingenuousness about his own self-interest with regard to the outcome of the lawsuit, nor even his tendency to paint the lawsuit in monochrome and cast everyone as us or them (I'm a "Sampas spy" according to Gerry, by the way), but his propensity for making Jan out to be a helpless victim. If she was a victim, the person who victimized her was herself. She was like her father in that respect. She had lots going for her: intelligence, good looks, street smarts. So her father and mother split up before she was born, and her mother, who was both phenomenally independent and phenomenally flaky, raised her in condemned buildings on the Lower East Side. So Jan came of age in the 1960s. So she dropped out of high school after her freshman year and did drugs and started drinking, got pregnant and fled the country. By and large, for about thirty years, Jan Kerouac did exactly what she wanted and got away with it.

For whatever reasons, in 1991 her past caught up with her and her kidneys gave out, and like her father, she died before her time. Yet despite the fact that she only met her father twice, she published two books of her own that frankly make her dad look like a stick-in-the-mud, although to my mind she had barely begun to develop her talent as a storyteller of her own life (a talent her father developed sublimely).

The person I got to know in the first three months of 1995 was already the wreck of a beautiful, tough New York girl. Her medicine cabinet overflowed with drugs to counteract the side effects of dialysis, and more drugs to counteract the side effects of those counteractants. My seven days in Jan Kerouac's presence were a visit to bedlam: a jaundiced woman of indeterminate age (sometimes she looked thirty-five, sometimes eighty-five), constantly picking at the fine hairs on her face, scratching her arms and hands with a hairbrush, springing up to swat at the mealy moths flying about the kitchen, complaining constantly of imperceptible odors ("I can smell one molecule of piss," she announced proudly). Afterward, I wondered how she kept herself together in public long enough to make an appearance, let alone be witty and entertaining, as she often was. But like any writer on a tour of hell, I couldn't help finding the psychological scenery fascinating.

I'll just say this: Jan could have made it, just like you and I made it through many of the same perils. Maybe she should have appealed to John Sampas's generosity after she came home from Puerto Rico in 1991. Maybe she should have distanced herself from her advisors, both legal and literary, as she appeared to do when the request to move Jack's body backfired in the media. Maybe she should have confided in her uncle, a stable, conservative, telephone-company executive. Maybe then she would still be alive and writing today. But hypothetical fallacy aside, if she had done all the right things, she wouldn't have been her father's daughter, or her mother's either, for that matter. And she certainly wouldn't have been the Jan Kerouac who enlivened hundreds of people's lives.

Her turn from life to death was ugly. But death is so insubstantial we can only appreciate it as a conclusion to life, finally a fullness rather than an emptiness. There are reasons for every crack-up, and we whet our appetite for destruction by trying to understand those reasons. We enjoy the crack-up itself most of all because it is our only modern version of tragedy. Like Janis and Jimi and Jim — perhaps even like Antigone — Jan succumbed not to the depredations of the Sampas family, but to her fate.

As of October 1998, Jan's lawsuit is hanging by a thread, kept alive only by Gerry Nicosia's final appeal to the New Mexico State Supreme Court. It revolves, curiously, around the question of whether the signature on Gabrielle Kerouac's will is forged. When Jack died, he hadn't even the good grace to mention his wife in his will, but left everything to his mother. Fortunately for Stella, Florida has dowry rights, so she automatically got a third of the estate. Another party in the lawsuit, though not of his own volition, is Paul Blake Jr., Jan's cousin, Jack Kerouac's sister's only child. In media accounts of the suit Paul is often conceived to be on the same side of the lawsuit as Jan. In fact, the cousins, though on friendly terms ever since Paul resurfaced about the time I got to know Jan, are legally adversaries. If Paul fails to pursue his own interest in his uncle's estate, Jan's heirs would presumably win two-thirds. But that is another story. The crucial argument over Kerouac's estate depended on whether a handwriting expert could be found to testify that Gabrielle's signature was forged and, further, whether the court would accept the expert testimony, as it seemed inclined to do when it reopened the probate in May 1994.

Jan never knew her granny, took little interest in legalities, and couldn't see well enough to notice anything irregular about a will she probably had never seen before. Who did notice a discrepancy? Someone with a financial stake in limiting John Sampas's control over the Kerouac archive, I'll venture to say. Jan's interest in preserving her father's papers for posterity was nothing more than a publicity slogan she learned to repeat. She had virtually no interest in scholarly matters; in fact, she hadn't even read most of her father's books. But she craved attention and enjoyed the status of minor celebrity. Even though her poetry and fiction are often appallingly dull, she took every opportunity to read before an audience of adoring (Jack) Kerouac fans. Someone with opportunity and (perhaps admirable) motives took it upon himself to suggest the possibility of forgery to Jan. Of course, she easily perceived her own advantage and wholeheartedly took up the banners prepared by her supporters.

The sad part of this is that the restriction of access to Kerouac's papers, reputedly begun by Stella after the publication of Ann Charters' biography (*Kerouac*, 1973), which has now become the central ethical issue surrounding the lawsuit, has been prolonged for several years by the lawsuit. If Jan had gained partial control of her father's estate, access might have been delayed indefinitely. The animosity created by the suit in two years may well have made it impossible for the joint owners even to speak to each other, let alone agree on a suitable site for the Kerouac collection.

As it now stands, Jan's heirs, David Bowers and John Lash, have agreed to drop the lawsuit, though Gerry Nicosia, who was named Jan's literary executor, has pursued it on his own behalf. While the lawsuit goes unresolved, we spectators are left to wonder just how this supposed forgery of Gabrielle's signature was effected. Did Stella Sampas, by all accounts a straightlaced, hardworking woman from a respectable family, suffer a moral lapse for fear of losing what little independence she had gained through her late marriage to an aging alcoholic with a demanding, invalid mother? Or was she coached by unscrupulous friends or relatives? Somehow, I just can't buy it. It's too much like a mystery novel. If we're going that route, why not fantasize that Stella also murdered both Jack and Gabrielle to escape her virtual household slavery and come away with little more than the title to a modest tract house in St. Petersburg? (Believe it or not, one of Jan's supporters actually phoned me once to report that he had found evidence that Jack was murdered. I told him to call the tabloids.)

No. Time for a strong dose of realism here. Somebody in the know, probably one or more of the several collectors who make money dealing in Kerouac manuscripts, tipped Gerry Nicosia to the irregularity of Gabrielle's signature, Gerry consulted his lawyer, Tom Brill, and when they decided they had a plausible case, Gerry renewed his fifteen-year acquaintance with Jan Kerouac. For all the reasons I've just discussed, Jan bought the story hook, line, and sinker, and she died in the hope that the two people she loved most in the world, John Lash and David Bowers, would profit from her quest to create a family, at least on legal-size paper.

TWO

JACK WED THREE WIVES

Just to put the story of Jan's life in perspective, her father married three times, at very different periods of his life, and for very different reasons, but always out of a distinct personal need. Like those between the spouses of most people who marry several times, the ties that bind Kerouac's three wives are not immediately apparent. The women differed widely in appearance, intelligence, character, and background. Yet they symbolize perfectly three distinct phases of Kerouac's life: the formative years of his early adulthood during World War II, the beginning of his life on the road, and his return to his hometown late in life to recreate the sense of stability and family he had lost in his wanderings.

First came Frankie "Edie" Parker, the daughter of a thrice-married Detroit woman, reared in some degree of affluence, thanks especially to her grandmother, who was the proximate cause of Edie's meeting Kerouac. When Edie quit high school about the time World War II broke out, she went to live with her grandma in Manhattan, near the Columbia and Barnard campuses. While studying art as a special student at Columbia, Edie fell in with a college crowd that included Henri Cru, a dashing young French American who had attended Columbia's prep school, Horace Mann. She also befriended a strange, cerebral young woman named Joan Vollmer, who later became the companion of William S. Burroughs. A wild young St. Louis aristocrat also joined this gang: Lucien Carr, shortly to become a legend of the early Beat circle.

Like Cru, Edie was not an intellectual, yet something drew her to intellectuals and artists, and likewise, something drew them to her. On their part, I imagine, it was her robust Midwestern good looks and animal spirit: Edie was a party girl, plain and simple. But she also knew how to take care of herself. In nothing I have read or heard about her do I detect anything but a strong sense of her own independence. On her part, I suppose, Burroughs, Carr, Ginsberg, and Kerouac offered a kind of adventure unavailable to a simple party girl: an exploration of the city as a kind of metaphysical exercise, a gathering of experience as the prelude to the creation of literature. In any case, Edie was, I believe, the glue that first cemented this unlikely combination of companions; if not the mother of the Beat Generation, she was at least its photo girl.

It was Cru who first introduced Edie to his former classmate and fellow francophone Jack Kerouac. Edie herself told the story, on film in 1982, without a trace of self-satire, of Jack's first impression of her. When they went for a snack, Edie voraciously downed six hot dogs. What virile young football player, steeped in the Freudian atmosphere of the Columbia campus, could fail to be impressed by such a feat? They became lovers. Edie introduced Jack around her circle, first to Lucien, whom Jack pegged right off as a "prick," then to Joan Vollmer, and thus to Burroughs, who came to him for information about work in the merchant marine. While Jack shipped out to Greenland and England on Liberty ships in 1942, Edie, characteristically, drove a dock train at the Brooklyn navy yard. According to her memoir, she conceived a child by Kerouac, a child that was aborted without his knowledge or consent. Throughout the war Edie and Jack (or Frankie and Johnnie, as they liked to call themselves as a couple, recalling the well-known murder ballad) kept up an on-again, off-again affair, Edie providing him with a place to stay in the city when he returned from a voyage or ventured in from his parents' apartment in Queens. She and Joan Vollmer, now Adams, took the large apartment that became the intensive salon, stage, and crash pad for the core of the Beat movement. But during these first years of wartime excitement and freedom, neither showed any inclination to marry. It was, ironically, Lucien Carr who led them — or rather forced them — to take that step.

Carr's 1944 murder of David Kammerer has become legendary in Beat lore. Suffice it to say, saving all the gory details for the next chapter, that Kammerer, a slightly older man who had been

Lucien's scout leader in St. Louis, conceived an unrequited love for the fair-haired boy, pursued it relentlessly by following him from boarding school to college, pressed his suit in New York by stalking and harassing Carr, and finally pushed his beloved over the boundary between annoyance and rage. Early one morning in a park by the Hudson River, Carr, goaded as he said by Kammerer's compulsive protestations of love, pulled out his trusty scout knife and stabbed his tormentor to death. Terrified by his own rash act, Lucien tried to weight the body down with rocks and send his old friend's corpse to the bottom of the river. Then he bethought himself of his best friend, traipsed over to Edie's apartment, climbed the fire escape, and opened the window on the sleeping lovers. Waking Jack with the dreadful news, Lucien asked for his help, making Kerouac an accessory after the fact to murder. After Jack dressed, the two men went back down the fire escape and off to get rid of the murder weapon and other evidence. Meanwhile, Edie slept on, blissfully unaware that this grisly sequence of events would serve as the rehearsal for her wedding.

After a long day, during which Jack and Lucien went to see a movie before Carr turned himself in (following Burroughs' advice), Kerouac was also arrested and held as a material witness. The cops were suspicious of what to them looked like a homosexual intrigue, and when they interrogated Jack, the gist of their questioning tended toward his sexual orientation. One detective assured his superior after a session with Kerouac in a cell that Jack was "a swordsman." Still, the authorities were forced to hold Jack in lieu of bail in connection with what the press began to call an "honor slaying." (Carr eventually spent two years in prison on manslaughter charges, after convincing the prosecutor that his actions were provoked by Kammerer's behavior.)

When Jack called his dad, a working-class conservative, Leo, infuriated that his son had besmirched the family name, refused to go his bail. Humiliated, Jack turned to his girlfriend, who in kind turned to her family. Mother and stepfather agreed to provide the cash — only $100 — on two conditions: first, that Jack and Edie get married; second, that Jack repay the money in six months. In short order Jack was taken out of his cell, escorted by the same detective, who served as his best man, to meet Edie before a judge, and married for the first time. Perhaps Kerouac was happy to prove his heterosexuality to the police, and thereby distance himself from Kammerer's involvement with Carr, because somehow the detective got the impression that Edie was pregnant. Not exactly a romantic wedding, but certainly the stuff of legend — at least Beat legend.

The bail money came from Detroit directly, and Jack was sprung, to the chagrin of his father. As promised, he determined to pay back the money as quickly as possible. The easiest way to do this seemed to the newlyweds to be to move to Detroit, where they could save rent by living with Edie's mother and sister. Jack got a job in a defense plant, set himself to study literary criticism (perhaps as a penance), and began to repay his debt to Edie's family. Unfortunately, he was miserable. Uncomfortable with the in-laws' lifestyle and missing the excitement of New York City, he paid the last installment of his loan, got on a bus, and returned to live with his parents.

Jack himself never seemed to be in any hurry to divorce either of his first two wives, but Edie — or her family — was not so casual about their parting. They hired a lawyer, who somehow convinced the Michigan court that an annulment was in order. And so in less than two years, Jack's first marriage had ended; however, the annulment made so little impression on Edie that forty years later she managed to forget about it, insisting to the Social Security Administration that she, rather than Stella Sampas Kerouac, deserved to receive the benefits owed to Jack Kerouac's widow. Nevertheless, in the late 1940s, Jack and Edie continued to see each other occasionally, and one of the scenes excised from the published version of On the Road describes Dean and Sal's visit to Detroit to visit Sal's ex-wife. Although Edie did get wind of the news of Jack's literary success in 1957, and it wasn't until just before he died and she was already twice remarried and twice more divorced that she renewed her interest in her first husband.

The case of Jack's second marriage, though more romantic than his first, is hardly a paradigm for success. For it too resulted from a desperate need, albeit of a very different kind from the need for bail money.

In the autumn of 1950, "coming home in October," as he liked to say, Jack Kerouac was well into his twenty-eighth year. His father had died in April 1946 of stomach cancer, and the event had prompted Kerouac to begin to take his work as a writer seriously. Shortly after Leo's death, Kerouac had been inspired by the entrance of Neal Cassady into his life, beginning what his fictional alter ego called his "life on the road." Jack's long autobiographical novel, *The Town and the City,* which ends with a painful Oedipal description of his father's death, had been published earlier in the year. And he was well into a draft of his first mature work and already contemplating a novel about his adolescence in Lowell.

But something was missing. His wandering, which he kept up all his life, often seemed to lack purpose. His mother had grown into middle age, and he had promised his father on his deathbed that he would take care of her. Their connections with their hometown grew more tenuous with the passage of time. Jack's sister, Caroline, had married a Southerner after the war, moved to North Carolina, and borne a son in 1948. Even his wild Western hero, Neal, had started a family and was making an attempt to settle down in California. Jack sensed it was time for him to marry again, this time for keeps. This sense preoccupied his thoughts, quickly generating a picture of an ideal wife — one who was both domestic and bohemian — and an ideal life, one that could be shared with both his mother and with Neal. A tall order which Joan Haverty clearly did not fill.

It is hard for me to accept at face value the legend of their first meeting. Joan, barely twenty years old, was induced to come to the city and introduced into bohemian circles by Jack's friend Bill Cannastra, a notorious Village daredevil with a Harvard law degree. Unbeknownst to Jack on his travels, Cannastra had recently been killed in a subway accident, and Joan was occupying his loft. One cool October evening, as she was fixing hot chocolate for her boyfriend, Herb, a shout came up from the street six stories below. It was Jack, looking either for Bill or for Lucien Carr, who lived nearby. Joan recognized the odd name, so she threw down the key, and before she knew it, Jack had sprinted up the stairs. Apparently, the sight of Joan, wearing a dress because her habitual dungarees were in the wash, stirring hot chocolate by the stove, rang chords of both memory and desire for Jack. Hadn't his mother treated him and his sister by making hot chocolate for them on just such frosty nights when they were kids? Was this thin, intelligent-looking, beautiful young woman the girl of his dreams? Jack seemed to think so. Though it seems unlikely that he was unaware of Joan's existence — why wouldn't he have heard of her, just as she had heard of him, through the grapevine? — there you have it. Another Beat legend: love at first sight, Greenwich Village style.

After ascertaining the disturbing news of Cannastra's death and obtaining a surreptitious disclaimer of Herb's serious attachment to Joan, Jack set about courting her in the same whirlwind fashion that he would shortly immortalize in his method of spontaneous composition. And like Carolyn Cassady before the importunings of Neal, Joan, who was only twenty at the time, was no proof against the blandishments of this handsome, young budding novelist. Within a month they were married, and by Christmas the newlyweds had moved in with Jack's mother, where he could get the kind of service he demanded of the woman of the house, a kind of service that Joan, to her credit, was unwilling to render. Early in 1951 she had already had enough of Jack's husbandly demands and criticism from his mother, so she offered him an ultimatum: she was going to find another apartment, and when the movers came for their things, he could either come with them, or stay with his mother. It was his choice.

When the moving truck arrived downtown, Jack was aboard, shepherding his writing desk along. He soon set to work at it in their new flat, and in April he produced the famous scroll manuscript of On the Road, after the Declaration of Independence, the most distinctive, if not the best-known manuscript in American literature, with the possible exception of Emily Dickinson's fascicle books. About this same time, Joan got pregnant, but instead of embracing the beginning of his dream of family life, Jack turned his back on it. The book was the child he dreamed of. Accusing Joan of sleeping with a Puerto Rican busboy (which she may well have done, given their bohemian lifestyle), Jack denied that he had fathered a child, perhaps to prevent his mother, a devout Catholic, from forcing him to remain married. Joan, for her part, seemed content to go her own way, though she naturally expected Jack to help with her medical bills and provide for her child. I am still troubled by accounts of their breakup in which Jack is said to have "abandoned" Joan. I expect there was mutual relief at their separation, she knowing as well as he that what they had done in haste, they could repent at leisure. That is not to deny that he hid from her in the years that followed.

Joan retreated to the refuge of her mother's home just south of Albany, where she came under the protection of her younger brother, Dave, who had just graduated from high school and gone to work for the telephone company. Jack, buoyed by the afflatus of his newly invented spontaneous prose and his newly developed sketching method of writing, began in earnest his most productive decade of writing, a decade he spent mostly on the lam, after Joan bore his only child, Janet Michele, on February 16, 1952. It took Joan years to chase him down, get the court to force him to take a blood test to compare to Jan's, and make him legally responsible for his daughter. He made his first payment ($52 per month) in 1961, when Jan was nine years old.

Like all minor tragedies of this sort, an unwanted child might be chalked up to youthful inexperience or recklessness. That may be the case for Joan, although my intuition tells me she was extremely mature for her age. As far as Jack Kerouac is concerned, however, the verdict is clear and harsh. He sacrificed his daughter, if not his wife, to his art. He chose perfection of the works over perfection of the life, as Yeats put it. While Joan developed into the kind of stubbornly independent and eccentric woman she wanted to be, Jan suffered from Jack's neglect, being simultaneously too much like him and too far distant from him to appreciate the danger of those fateful genetic similarities.

After his brief second marriage Jack again showed little inclination to sever their legal ties. It took Joan's initiative, spurred by a second pregnancy in 1957, to obtain a Mexican divorce, granted the summer before the first edition of On the Road hit the bookstores and the first Beat craze began. For all practical purposes, however, Jack remained unmarried from mid-1951 until 1966, just three years before his death. In this fifteen-year period, of course, he had several significant relationships with women, two of whom have written revealing memoirs. Carolyn Cassady contributes her intimate insight into Kerouac's love life by describing her ménage à trois with him and her husband, Neal, in the period immediately following the breakup of Jack's marriage to Joan. The hallmark of this *Off the Road* relationship is the clear desire, at least on Kerouac's part, to merge the roles of girlfriend, wife, and mother. What Jack seemed to want most — his ideal, let's say — was an extended family in which he could express his love for another man by making love to that man's wife.

Later in the 1950s, at the exact moment of the rise to fame that proved to be his undoing, Jack formed a relationship with a much younger woman. As she herself explains thoughtfully in *Minor Characters*, Joyce Johnson presented Kerouac with an interesting dilemma. By this time he was in his mid-thirties, and most of his best writing was behind him. Ahead lay many minor debacles of his alcoholic demise. But Johnson was herself an aspiring novelist who eventually achieved success as an editor and writer. At first helpful and encouraging about her career, Jack was clearly baffled by this young woman's desire to engage in his profession. By this time, he had also begun to act upon his promise to his father to take care of his mother, and now less than ever could he separate the role of son from that of husband. Rather than take up the responsibilities of his own fatherhood, he fled from them, becoming, in effect, both husband and son to his mother and leaving his girlfriend in the lurch. Joyce Johnson was another of the women who gained an intimate perspective on this Oedipal drama as Kerouac acted it out.

During this fifteen-year period between his second and third marriages, Kerouac found a surrogate family at his sister Nin's home, first in North Carolina and later in Florida. As Jack slowly but inevitably slipped into the role of husband to his own mother, he also found a surrogate son in Nin and Paul's boy, his nephew, Paul Blake Jr. Presumably, Jack poured out on Little Paul all the affection he withheld from his own daughter. Perhaps the aspect of Kerouac's life most neglected by biographers is this relationship with his sister and her family. Nin, in fact, is carefully backgrounded by Kerouac himself in all his writing except *Doctor*

Sax. Paul Junior, who loved and revered his mother, recalls details of the Kerouac family life that appear nowhere in print. His recollection of his Uncle Jack suggests that he too was aware of the important role he and his mother played in Jack's life. Carolyn's death in 1964 precipitated the stroke that disabled her mother for the last years of her life, and according to Paul, the loss of Nin also destroyed what remained of Jack's weakened will to live. Even then, when Paul was already a teenager, the strong bond remained between nephew and uncle. So far as anyone can determine, Paul Blake Jr. was the last person Jack wrote to before he died.

Carolyn's death, Gabrielle's disability, and Jack's failing spirits combined to precipitate his third and last marriage, to Stella Sampas, the older sister of one of his boyhood pals, which betrays yet another kind of need, perhaps the most desperate of all: the inability to care for someone who had always taken care of him and the need to find someone trustworthy to fill that role of caregiver. Yet this relationship has its romance as well as its pathos, for according to Sampas family legend, Stella had always loved Jack, ever since they were teenagers together in Lowell in the 1930s. Further, to this day, members of her family continue to assert that Stella "saved herself" for Jack — something he also told at least one friend — and that their wedding day marked the fulfillment of her fondest dreams. I see no reason to question that legend, though I suspect Kerouac's motives and feelings differed dramatically from those of his last wife. In any case, Jack always kept up his correspondence with Stella, even going so far as to explain to her the failure of his marriage to Joan and to express his hope that he could marry again and settle with his wife and mother in Lowell.

Stella herself was quite different from both of Jack's other wives. Though she was perfectly intelligent and capable, her father had forced her to leave high school during the Depression to help her mother care for the younger Sampas children. As the oldest daughter, Stella thus assumed the role of surrogate mother even before she emerged from girlhood. In the early 1970s she told Barry Gifford that Jack had proposed to her before he married Joan, but Stella refused him because she "had a family to raise."

In this sense, though she could not have known it, she acquired the best possible training for her married life. Learning how to manage a large household in bad economic times, however, did not prevent her from also learning in other ways. When the family fortunes improved and her brothers began to go off to college, she checked out copies of the books they read for their classes so she could discuss them when the boys came home on break. After Jack's death, Stella wrote intelligent and sympathetic letters — even a few to Edie — in which she frequently quoted lines of poetry.

Indeed, Stella almost seems cut from the cloth of the previous century. Raised in a Victorian atmosphere in which sex was never even mentioned, let alone discussed, she was about as far from being a bohemian as you can possibly get. And perhaps this antiquated sense of propriety served her in good stead when her girlhood crush returned to propose marriage, for by 1966 Jack was in full flight from the counterculture he was thought to have spawned. Not only did he attempt to return to Lowell in both body and spirit, but he actually came to resemble his fictional descriptions of his own father. Stella completed the revised family portrait: she was the middle-aged version of the hometown girl Jack wrote about in *Maggie Cassidy*, the girl he wanted to marry in 1939, but couldn't because of his ambition.

Stella is often blamed for refusing to allow scholars to peruse Jack's unpublished writings, but her supposed reason — her shock that Ann Charters inquired so closely into her deceased husband's sex life in her 1973 biography — makes perfect sense in light of her upbringing. And while the still-restricted access to Kerouac's papers became the main issue in the battle for control of the estate, I can't see that Stella's reserve has damaged Kerouac's reputation, except in academic circles, where the availability of letters, notes, diaries, drafts, and marginalia counts for a lot. He's more popular in the 1990s than ever.

So after twenty years of keeping house on Stevens Street, Stella emerged to go to work outside the home in various shoe shops in Lowell. The poster for the 1995 Lowell Celebrates Kerouac! conference, an annual get-together of local experts and fans and scholars from all over the world, featured a snapshot of her taken on a beach in Greece in 1965. While Stella looks pleased to be standing on the soil of her ancestors' homeland, the exuberance of youth is lost to her. Her eyes betray her own sense that she has missed the boat in some sense, and that grateful appreciation will have to serve in place of excitement.

I wonder what her feelings were on her wedding day. If, as the family stories have it, she had saved herself for Jack for thirty years, what could she expect but disappointment? How could any reality live up to that many years of expectation? But the correspondence between Jack and Stella had never lapsed in all those years, and as I say, she was not stupid. Tempered by long service to her own family, she may have entered marriage with the idea of becoming caregiver to an adopted set of relatives. Still I sometimes shudder to think of the indignities heaped on her by a demanding old lady and a drunken novelist. Especially considering the reports of Jack's arguments with his mother, which apparently often took the form of gross mutual sexual insults.

But Stella bore it bravely and patiently, perhaps even stoically. She outlived her husband by more than twenty years, her invalid mother-in-law by more than fifteen. She lived long enough to see a rather elaborate monument erected in Jack's memory in 1988 in a small park in downtown Lowell. And perhaps she lived long enough to see that her own estate would bear the fruit of her long-suffering nature: that the effects of her late husband — literary, artistic, and personal — would be valued in the millions of dollars and that after her death she would still be helping to take care of her younger brothers and sisters in their old age.

In a strange way Stella turned Jack's desperation and delusion to her own advantage. While she was never rich in the 1970s or 1980s, the royalties from Jack's books finally began to provide her with more than a subsistence income. In 1983 Jan Kerouac came forward to make her first claim on those royalties, and for the last five years of her life, Stella shared the money with her estranged stepdaughter. I doubt if she felt any rancor over that, because she seemed to want those who deserved to be taken care of to profit from Jack's growing fame. But she drew the line in a family sort of way, and biographers and scholars are not family. Jack must have known that his years were numbered when he married

Stella. I like to think that in choosing her for his last wife, he not only satisfied his own pressing needs at the time, but also contrived to fix the focus of his life in Lowell rather than on the road. For better or worse, Stella's inheritance of the Kerouac estate and her handling of it emphasized to the outside world that in Lowell family still comes first, and Jack Kerouac is now a member of the Sampas family.

THREE

YOU'LL BE OKAY

On a cold October day in 1982, Jim Perrizo was browsing in one of his favorite used bookstores in Detroit when he heard the phone ring. Mary Taylor, the owner of Grub Street Books, answered, and Jim turned back to his pursuit of authors from the Beat Generation. After a few minutes Mary beckoned him to the phone. When he reached her desk, she said, "There's someone on the phone I want you to meet. It's Jack Kerouac's first wife."

Serendipity strikes everyone's life, but for a young man who had devoted much of his time in graduate school to the unappreciated area of what is now called Beat Studies, this chance connection with Edie Parker, one of the original cast of characters in the drama that unfolded near the Columbia University campus at the beginning of World War II, represented a dream come true. Of course, he knew she still lived in the Detroit area, thanks to the occasional articles by a local journalist and Kerouac fan in the *Free Press*, but Jim had never tried to contact her. Edie had just returned to her hometown from a trip to the Soviet Union with her boyfriend, but where Jim was concerned, even travel as interesting as that took a backseat to Edie's participation in the previous summer's celebration of the twenty-fifth anniversary of the publication of *On the Road* at the Naropa Institute in Boulder, Colorado, an event marking the end of one epoch in Beat Studies and the beginning of another, officially inaugurating Kerouac's status as a cult figure. As he took the receiver from Mary Taylor, however, Jim could not possibly imagine the sequence of events that would enmesh him for a while in Edie's life and then cast him out of that life with a mixed inheritance of bitterness, dismay, and relief.

In very short order after that first phone call, Edie began to recognize Jim's talent for assimilating and synthesizing information about her famous first husband, and by the following year he had begun to type and copy materials for her (still unpublished) memoir, *You'll Be Okay*. In the summer of 1986 he succeeded two previous secretaries as Edie's boy Friday.

I first met Jim and Edie about a year after that, at the River City Reunion, another of the periodic self-styled Beat revivals, this one with the unlikely venue of Lawrence, Kansas, where William S. Burroughs had taken up residence at the behest of his secretary, James Grauerholz. One of the first things I noticed about Edie's public statements was that they had a suspiciously canned ring, as though they had been scripted. Not just canned, either, but familiar. I got the nagging feeling that I had read her words somewhere before, though I knew that was impossible. Almost nine years later, when I made contact with Jim in the process of writing this book, he solved the mystery for me. Most of what Edie said after Jim became her secretary was what he had coached her to say, based on his own careful reading of the several biographies of Jack Kerouac. So if some of what Edie said on stage in 1987 sounded as though Gerry Nicosia had scripted it, that was because of Jim's diligent attempts to prevent Edie from reinventing her past. His scrupulousness, however, eventually led him into conflict with her.

In 1996 Jim was kind enough to send me copies of much of the material he and Edie had developed in the course of their work together, and so the version of Edie's life that follows is theirs, although of course with Jim as my exemplar, I've done the same kind of cross-checking he did before me.

Frankie Edith ("Edie") Parker was born September 20, 1922, six months after the man who was destined to become her first husband. Her parents were Charlotte Maire Gordon, the daughter of a prominent Grosse Pointe physician and widow of the owner of Gordon's Ground-Gripper Shoes in Detroit and Buffalo, and Walter Parker, a New York playboy, sportsman, and businessman, not necessarily in that order. Her parents' marriage, like their fortune, was ruined by Walter's drinking, and in 1941, they divorced. Tomboyish Edie, who had artistic inclinations, convinced her mother that she could get much better training in New York City, and Charlotte, perhaps to ease the strain of the breakup of her marriage on both herself and her daughter, allowed Edie to move in with her paternal grandparents. The elder Parkers had an apartment in the Fairmount overlooking the garden of Nicholas Murray Butler, the president of Columbia University, which was just across Amsterdam Avenue. Supported by her mother, who continued to operate the family shoe business until she remarried (to Joseph Sharrard), and by her doting grandmother, for whom she was named, Edie proceeded to act the role of the spoiled rich kid loose in the big city.

One of her first discoveries was the West End Bar, a hangout for Columbia undergraduates, including the football players and, after Pearl Harbor, military cadets. Soon she was playing hooky from her high school classes in order to cadge drinks at the West End, and finally she gave up the pretense of going to school altogether. Somehow, she missed meeting Jack Kerouac that year. Jack's only full year at Columbia was the 1940–41 academic year. In the fall of 1941 he quit the football team to work a series of odd jobs, traveling first to Washington, DC, then returning north to join his parents, who were then living in New Haven, and finally moving back to Lowell with them. Besides, Edie was still attached to her Grosse Pointe friends and to kids she met during the summer at her grandparents' summer home in North Asbury Park, New Jersey. In fact, a prank Edie pulled in Asbury Park got her shipped home after just a few months in the Big Apple. On Halloween 1941, without asking permission, Edie went over to New Jersey and opened the house there for a party for her friends. Naturally, Gram (as they called the old lady) found out, and Edie was sent packing back to the Midwest.

Edie's grandfather died the next summer, and to ease Gram's transition into widowhood, Charlotte allowed her older daughter to return to New York, perhaps against her better judgment. This time Edie gave up trying to finish high school; rather, she worked different jobs made available by the burgeoning war effort and began to party in earnest. As Jim Perrizo noted, Edie was always the leader of the pack, "not a delinquent, but always in search of adventure." Adventure, for her, seemed to come in the form

of boyfriends, many different boyfriends. Upon her return to
New York, she met almost immediately a twenty-two-year-old
French-American boy — Gram thought he looked like Tyrone
Power and adored his manners — named Henri Cru, the son of a
Columbia professor.

Henri, or Hank, as Edie called him, had little interest in academics or in the war effort, although he had attended Horace
Mann and intended to enlist in the merchant marine. One of his
younger buddies at the prep school was now a Columbia football
player, although he seemed unable to get along with the well-
known head coach, Lou Little. Soon Hank had introduced Edie to
his fellow French American, none other than Jack Kerouac, who
had just returned from a three-month voyage to Greenland on
the S.S. *Dorchester*. Impressed by her upper-middle-class confidence and style — Edie often sang for her friends at the bar —
Jack asked her if she wanted to go across the street to a deli for a
snack, and there, much to his amazement, Edie consumed six
sauerkraut hot dogs. That feat amply demonstrated her appetite
for more than food, and by November Jack and Edie were screwing on the red velvet couch in Gram's living room, while the old
lady, already deaf as a stone, slept peacefully in her bedroom.

Edie wasn't above crass treatment of Jack, however. She copied
his first love letter to her and sold the copies for a dollar apiece
to lovelorn navy cadets at Columbia later that winter. And apparently their lovemaking escaped Hank's notice, because well into
the next year he labored under the illusion that he and Edie were
engaged, perhaps encouraged by Gram's favor. At about the
same time as she first started sleeping with Jack, Edie also met
another Columbia football player, Charlie Singer, whom she also
began to date without telling either Jack or Henri. This pattern
continued throughout Jack and Edie's relationship, both of them
sleeping with other partners, even while they were married.

Consequently, when Edie discovered she was pregnant just
before Christmas, she could not be certain who the father was,
although in later years she revised her uncertainty into literary
history by claiming the child was Jack's. Though no documentary
proof of the abortion remains, Edie's younger sister (whom
everyone called Sister to distinguish her from her namesake,

Charlotte, her mother) was on the scene at the time and testifies to Gram's horror when she discovered Edie's condition. Edie also believed that the abortion, performed of course illegally at that time, made her sterile, and it is a fact that though she married three times in her life, she bore no children.

At the time of her abortion in late January 1943, all her boyfriends were away, and Edie had to endure the operation alone. Jack was engaged in his ill-fated attempt to join the navy, which eventually landed him in the mental ward at Bethesda Naval Hospital, from which he was unceremoniously but honorably discharged. In his biography *Memory Babe*, Gerry Nicosia places the abortion in the summertime, perhaps because that's when Jack returned to the city, found Edie, and learned of her calamity. With her typical healthful resilience, by March she had recovered sufficiently to land a job driving heavy equipment at the Brooklyn Navy Yard. Though "officially" continuing to reside with Gram, with her first paycheck Edie rented a room in an apartment leased by her friend Joan Vollmer Adams, another acquaintance she had met at the West End, in this case a Barnard student from Albany who was noted for reading all the editions of all the local newspapers every day. In this apartment, shared by one woman who had just undergone an abortion and another woman soon to be impregnated by a husband home briefly on leave (Paul Adams was serving in the army), the Beat Generation was born.

It was at this time, summer of 1943, that Jack developed another habit that lasted for the next ten years or more. After helping his parents move from Lowell to Ozone Park in Queens, where work was more plentiful, he began to split his time between weekdays with Edie in the city and weekends with Leo and Gabrielle. Though he seemed perfectly satisfied during his nights with Edie, and though he often managed to write in the apartment while she was at work, Edie must have been troubled by his continuing dependence on his parents. Her suspicions were raised further when Jack announced his intention to ship out again, and in July he left her high and dry as he sailed on the S.S. *Weems*, bound for Liverpool with a cargo of explosives. By the time he returned three months later, she had not only changed jobs, but she and Joan had moved down a block to 421 West 118th Street, Apt. 62.

Now began the only year that could truly be called Edie and Jack's life together.

In late October Edie called her sister to announce her intention to marry Jack, and a few days later she took him home to meet her parents. Her mother found herself unimpressed with this taciturn, though admittedly good-looking fellow from New England. Walter, on the other hand, found in Jack a willing drinking partner and took a shine to him. In November Jack reciprocated by taking Edie to visit his hometown, although they ran out of cash and Edie's mother had to wire money to Lowell so the couple could return to New York. Jack abandoned Edie at Christmas, however, preferring still to spend the holiday alone with his parents, although he did return to the city for New Year's Eve, celebrating with Edie, Sister, and another of his old prep-school pals, a young Englishman named Seymour Wyse, who had encouraged and educated Jack's interest in jazz beginning in 1939.

In the first weeks of the new year Gram somehow discovered that Edie had been forced to obtain the lease on her and Joan's apartment by enlisting Jack's help and signing it in the name of Mr. and Mrs. Jack Kerouac. This bit of harmless subterfuge hurt not only her grandmother, but her mother as well. Following the previous year's abortion, the news that her daughter was officially living in sin prompted Charlotte to write Edie a series of sermonizing letters, admonishing her to go to church, respect herself, restrain her appetites, and live up to her good breeding. If she had only known, in this case the reality was far worse than the appearance.

For in January 1944 Edie had enrolled as a special student at Columbia in order to pursue her interest in art, and in her first drawing class she made the acquaintance of a rakish lad only recently arrived from St. Louis. Lucien Carr's exploits had already gained the notice of upperclassmen at the West End, and his pursuit by a homosexual admirer became both the proximate cause of Jack and Edie's marriage and the grist for one of the most sensational Beat legends. Lucien soon introduced Edie to his precocious classmate Allen Ginsberg, the son of a New Jersey high school English teacher who had already determined on a career as a union lawyer.

On his renewed weekday visits after the holidays, Jack, bristling with lower-middle-class paranoia, took an instant dislike to both boys, the Midwesterner and the Jew, but his first impression was soon reversed by the stimulation of their companionship. In short order, a mutual acquaintance of these new friends, a cadaverous older fellow named William S. Burroughs, turned up at the apartment in search of Jack, from whom he wished to obtain information about joining the merchant marine. Later, though his sexual leanings were predominantly homosexual, Burroughs joined Joan Adams in what has to be one of the most bizarre marriages in the history of civilization.

Oddly, though Edie's gregarious nature served as the catalyst for the creation of the Beat Generation, she was, to use a ready-made phrase, in it but not of it. She was intelligent but not intellectual, artistic but not an artist, promiscuous but not orgiastic, adventurous but not self-destructive. And she soon discovered to her own chagrin that the gang she had brought together often disgusted her with their extravagant behavior.

In the meantime, however, Joan decided that it would be safer and more secure for her to deliver her first child with the help of her parents, who lived in Loudonville, a suburb of Albany, and in April she left to prepare for the arrival of the baby, expected in June. Jack was feeling the wanderlust after six months on shore, and in May he left for New Orleans to try to catch a ship. As he was returning circuitously (by way of Asheville, North Carolina, birthplace of his literary idol, Thomas Wolfe, and Washington, DC, where one of his high school buddies from Lowell was still working a construction job at the new Pentagon building), Edie started to date Lucien's Columbia roommate, John Kingsland, if only to make Jack jealous when he finally got back to New York. But after the spring term ended, things quieted down around Columbia and Jack and Edie settled into a comfortable routine, she working and he writing. He even began to take her out to Queens on the weekends to visit his parents. Often after one of Gabrielle's home-cooked dinners, the two couples went out for drinks or to catch a movie. Although Jack's parents were as concerned about appearances as Edie's mom, they liked Edie, perhaps because she was simple, lively, and fun-loving —

their own kind of people — or perhaps just because she seemed extraordinarily normal compared to Jack's other new friends, whom his parents mostly despised.

Jack and Edie spent most of the summer living their amusing, if unconventional, life and enjoying the relative peace of the big apartment. Until very early one morning in mid-August, when Lucien Carr paid them a most unexpected visit. Lucien himself was far from conventional in his behavior, so at first Jack and Edie were not too surprised to find that he had climbed up the fire escape, let himself in through a window, and entered their bedroom as they slept in the sweltering pre-dawn of the summer city. But there all certainties ceased.

As Lucien shook Jack awake, Edie also came to understand drowsily that something horrible had happened. What was it? At first, she couldn't make it out. Then, gradually, like a nightmare remembered in bits and snatches, it came clear. During an early morning walk in Riverside Park, David Kammerer, the man who had pursued — stalked, we would say today — Lucien for several years, had propositioned him in a threatening way. Lucien, probably drunk, took Kammerer's offer as a fatal ultimatum, they scuffled, and in the heat of the moment Lucien pulled out his Boy Scout knife and stabbed his would-be lover repeatedly until he was dead. As if that weren't bad enough, in the aftermath of his deed Lucien had weighted the body and pushed it into the Hudson. Paradoxically, he had neglected to dispose of less bulky evidence, including Kammerer's bloodstained eyeglasses and the murder weapon. Now he needed Jack's help to conclude his cover-up.

Apparently, Jack, who was usually fairly cautious about avoiding the authorities, felt some guilt about what had happened, in that he had told Kammerer of Lucien's whereabouts after bumping into him the previous evening, so he rushed to dress and went off with his friend against his — and Edie's — better judgment. In doing so he soon became an accessory after the fact in a homicide, and by the end of the day Lucien had been arrested for murder and Jack had been jailed as a material witness in the case. For her part, Edie simply had to go to work at her defense job, where she spent the day in turmoil, wondering about the outcome of her lover's rash decision.

Much of what happened in the aftermath of Kammerer's death seems strange by today's standards, but the America of the 1950s was naively and straightforwardly repressive. The cops who interviewed Kerouac were obviously more interested in determining whether he was straight or gay than in establishing his connection to the murderer and the murder. Edie came in handy in this respect, but she also wound up providing the bail money, which she could obtain only after she and Jack were married.

First of all, Jack had called his parents, but his father, who disliked most of his city friends, flipped when Jack told him why he was in jail. To have his son mixed up in a homosexual murder confirmed Leo's worst fears, and he simply exploded. No, he would not bail Jack out. He had disgraced the family name and he could rot in prison, as far as Leo was concerned. Instinctively, Jack turned to Edie, who had money in her family, even if her mother was not rich. Edie phoned Gram, who had a rather low opinion of Jack from the start, and Gram informed her that the terms of her husband's will were clear: the money he left in trust for his granddaughters could be released only upon their marriage. Edie phoned her mother. Given the disappointing turn in Edie's behavior since she first came to New York, and especially in light of her immorality in the past two years, Charlotte might easily have reacted as Leo did. But she didn't. Edie pleaded her love for Jack, and Charlotte opted for realpolitik. Here, at best, was an opportunity to make an honest woman of her daughter. She gave Edie her blessing, hoping to make the best of a bad situation. She would loan her the money for Jack's bail using for collateral the money from Edie's share of her grandfather's estate.

Within days of the murder, Edie, in the company of Celine Young, Lucien's girlfriend, found herself in a New York courtroom. Jack was led in by a homicide detective, who also served as a witness to the marriage. After the "I do's" Jack went back to the Tombs, and Edie went to phone Gram, who set in motion the legal machinery to release Edie's trust fund. In a few more days, $100 cash from her mother in hand, she bailed her new husband out of jail. By this time Leo, badgered by his wife, had relented, and the Kerouac side of the new family also accepted that perhaps everything had happened for the best, although it was hard to see it so soon. Besides, Leo and Gabe actually liked Edie.

When the New York papers got hold of Lucien's story, they put a 1950s spin on it, calling it an "honor slaying." That is, Lucien had killed in self-defense to preserve his purity from an assault by a homosexual. Burroughs' advice to the young man had also helped. Lucien had turned himself in voluntarily, and his mother, who now also lived in Manhattan, hired a good lawyer. Balancing Lucien's family background against Kammerer's history of stalking him, the district attorney reduced the charge from first-degree murder to involuntary manslaughter, and Jack was off the hook. Coincidentally, the lease was almost up on their apartment, so the new Mr. and Mrs. Kerouac fled to Detroit, where they could live cheaply with Edie's mother while the heat died down.

Before they left town, however, Jack and Edie went to Ozone Park to spend the Labor Day weekend with Jack's parents. From here, Jack wrote a formal letter to Charlotte stating his honorable intentions toward Edie, promising to pay back the money she had advanced to pay his bail, and laying down a diplomatic foundation for the joining of their two families. Apparently anticipating some tension, he assured his new mother-in-law that her "notions about life and morals" accorded closely with those of his father. He concluded philosophically but inappropriately, "In a world where death is rampant, as today, marriage is the least evil — that much is certain."

Ironically, the legalization of their relationship proved to be its undoing. Jack realized at once how uncomfortable he was around Edie's upper-middle-class friends and relations, and he must have foreseen a future cut to her specifications rather than his own. Jack's mother wrote to tell them she missed them, and enclosed a clipping describing the latest developments in Lucien's case, but by the end of September Jack had returned to find a ship in New York, which he did, though it turned out to be an unsatisfactory one. By this time Joan Adams had returned to the city with her newborn daughter, Julie, and found another apartment on West 115th Street. She wrote to Detroit asking Edie or her mom to pay the last utility bill from the previous place, which Jack and Edie had neglected in their haste to leave town. Since Joan's credit was tied up with theirs, she couldn't get service. So Edie was temporarily persona non grata with her old roommate. Meanwhile, after an encounter with a nasty first mate aboard the S.S. *Robert Treat Paine*, Jack jumped ship in Norfolk and made his way back to New York, crashing first in a Columbia dorm room with Allen Ginsberg, then with Burroughs on Riverside Drive, and finally moving with him into Joan's apartment, where Edie joined them briefly two weeks before Christmas.

This failed attempt at reconciliation must have distracted Edie, because early in January 1945 she was involved in a near-fatal car crash in Detroit, which brought Jack out for a visit. His heart was more than ever with his friends, however, and he went back to resume his double life in the city, splitting his time between Joan's place and his parents' apartment in Ozone Park. And though Edie told everybody, including herself, that she wanted to save her marriage, before she had even recovered from her accident she started dating a local guy named Ewart "Smitty" Smith. Even after she felt well enough to follow Jack to New York, she continued to see Smitty. To alleviate the confusion, Jack offered to divorce Edie so she could marry her new beau, but she refused, apparently still believing she could make Jack jealous and so get him to toe the line. Unwelcome to live at Joan's, Edie opted to spend the summer with Gram in Asbury Park, where Jack wrote to her regularly. Edie refused either to answer his messages or to meet him in the city unless he sent her money. But there was trouble on the homefront, and after a brief stint at a summer camp, Jack turned his attention to his family: Leo had been diagnosed with stomach cancer.

When fall came, Edie decided to try one last gambit. She convinced Joan that she would make up for last year's financial irresponsibility by working in the city to pay the rent on Joan's new place. The scene there had deteriorated badly (to Edie's way of thinking) since Bill Burroughs moved in. The place was always filled with a mixture of new Columbia undergraduates and seedy street punks. And everybody there was getting high. The latest fad was abusing Benzedrine inhalers, and Joan herself took the lead in these marathon speed sessions. Sometimes it made Edie's skin crawl, but she determined to make one last effort to rescue Jack from a life of degradation and turn him into a decent, upstanding, wage-earning husband. Edie got a job as a cigarette girl in a nightclub, and frequently when she came home after work at 4 AM, the gang was going full tilt, with Bill and Joan competing for the intellectual spotlight and Jack, wide-eyed with his buzz, taking it all in.

One day Joan's husband showed up unexpectedly on leave. Disgusted by the chaotic conditions in which he found his wife and daughter, he left muttering his disbelief that he had just fought a war to preserve such a way of life. He never returned. Pretty soon, Edie had had her fill as well. She gave Jack an ultimatum: come back to Detroit with her or call it quits. Jack opted for the subculture, and even if he had changed his mind, the wages of sin soon prevented him from leaving: the Benzedrine abuse caused blood clots to form in his legs. In December he entered the VA hospital in Queens, diagnosed with the first of several flare-ups of thrombophlebitis, the same disease that plagued Richard Nixon. Edie joined her sister at home for Christmas, recalling ruefully that in all their time together she and Jack had never spent a Christmas in the same home.

Edie was never one to pine for a lost lover, however, and even though Jack might have been the love of her life, she soon found other interests, namely in the person of Dick Sahlin, a wealthy young Grosse Pointer whose family disapproved of Edie. She landed a job in Detroit and began to date Dick steadily. She gradually drew away from Jack, who wrote in April with the news that Leo had died at home in Jack's presence. Later he claimed that his father's death had turned him into a serious writer. From his collaboration with Burroughs on a novel about the Lucien Carr/David Kammerer incident, Jack reverted to an independent project that ultimately became his first published novel, *The Town and the City*. In order to cement her relationship with Dick Sahlin, Edie went to the family lawyer, who managed somehow to finagle an annulment from the Wayne County court. As of September 1946 Edie Parker's two-year marriage to Jack Kerouac officially ceased to exist.

One of the qualities that makes *The Town and the City* fascinating reading, at least for present purposes, is the portrait it paints of Edie and Jack's relationship. Kerouac renders the tensions between them in frank detail. There are intellectual and artistic disparities, but the root of most of Judie Smith's and Peter Martin's disagreements is class, and though he allows Peter to express some of his prejudice against her middle-class background, Kerouac is brave enough to put Judie's case in a good light some of the time. For instance, late in the novel when she is trying to win Peter away from his shady friends, he asks her, "Judie, who do you think I am — a Rockefeller?" He continues: "I haven't got any money. I don't know what I'm going to do, and I don't want to be tied down." Judie responds with both anger and resignation: "You'll understand some day, because there won't be another woman around who'll understand you the way I do. Remember that! You're awful dumb, Pete, so awful dumb. Any other woman would laugh at you, you'll find out that after I've gone away."

Whether Kerouac himself ever found it out remains uncertain, although his later correspondence with Edie seems to indicate as much, but in any case, after 1946 their lives diverged as radically as two American lives might. Jack proceeded into the decade of writing that finally brought him notoriety — if not fame — with the publication of *On the Road* in 1957, and after a few more false starts, Edie found a man willing to marry her and stay. In fact, she found two such men, though apparently neither one ever lived up to the financial expectations she had of Jack.

After stints in secretarial school in East Lansing, about the time her mother remarried, and at a flower-arranging school in Boston, Edie married Mike Dietz, a local Detroit golf pro. Almost immediately after they moved to Florida, however, the couple began to have difficulty getting along. Mike, who was a Catholic, pressured Edie into getting an official religious annulment of her first marriage from the Detroit curia. This dispensation was granted in 1952, but her second marriage broke up in the autumn of 1954. When *On the Road* came out, Edie was unattached, so she wrote Jack and invited herself along on the round-the-world book promotion tour she assumed he was going to make, but

Jack was too busy being lionized by the New York literary estab-
lishment. Besides, he already had a female companion, Joyce
Glassman (Johnson). In 1959 Edie married Pat Garvin, and this
time she stayed married for ten years, although she supported
herself by acting as caretaker of the estate of her stepfather,
Joseph Sharrard, where she and her husband made their home.
Just two weeks before Edie's third marriage officially ended, Jack
Kerouac died.

In 1968 Charlotte Pattison, Edie's sister, who lived in Massachusetts not far from Lowell, saw a notice for a new Kerouac novel
called *Vanity of Duluoz*. When she picked it up and read it,
Charlotte, who was on the scene with Edie during the war,
realized that Kerouac's most recent novel was, in fact, a revision
of his first published book, *The Town and the City*, so she sent
Edie a copy. There, in the midst of a text dedicated and addressed
to Stella Sampas, Edie found a second recounting of her life with
Jack. It must have been a strange sensation to read as Jack Duluoz
explained to his third wife how he had met and married his
first wife.

"In those days," Kerouac wrote, Edie (whom he called Johnnie
in the novel, reversing the names of the ballad characters, Frankie
and Johnnie) "looked about what Mamie Van Doren looks like
today, same build, height, with the same almost buck-toothed
grin, that eagering grin and laugh and eagerness entire that
makes the eyes slit but at the same time makes the cheeks fuller
and endows the lady with the promise that she will look good all
her life." Such tenderness undoubtedly gave Edie a nostalgic
rush, and she set about reestablishing contact with Jack, who
hadn't written her since 1957, the year *On the Road* was published, when he was about to leave for Tangiers to visit Burroughs.

Edie's renewed interest in Kerouac soon led to phone conversations with him, and in September 1969 he wrote to invite her
to St. Petersburg, Florida, where he was living with Stella and his
invalid mother. He had just gotten beat up in a local bar and
thrown in jail. He reported that he was too sick to come to
Detroit, but that if Edie could scrounge up the fare, she was
welcome to visit them. He knew Stella wouldn't approve, but
he insisted that both he and his mother wanted to see Edie so

they could talk old times. He followed this with a telegram and another letter near the end of the month. This was followed by ominous silence, however, and Edie, who was preoccupied with the finalization of her second divorce, failed to notice the lapse. Then, on October 26, she got the news that Jack was dead, a victim of his own heavy drinking. The funeral would be held in Lowell in just a few days, and Edie resolved to attend.

Charlotte picked her up in Boston, and together they drove the short distance to Jack's hometown. Because of some confusion about Jack's home parish, he was buried out of the big church on Moody Street, St. Jean Baptiste, rather than out of the basement sanctuary of St. Louis de France in the Centralville neighborhood where he grew up. Regardless, the event proved to be a meeting of the two cultures Jack celebrated in the two novels in which Edie figures prominently: the home folks of Lowell, both Greek and French-American, and the Beat rebels and artists from his life in bohemia. Many of the people Edie had introduced him to came up for the service, most notably Allen Ginsberg, who appeared in his 1960s incarnation, replete with scraggly hair and beard. Since Edie last saw him, Allen had become a pop-culture icon himself, and his public appearances, publishing success, and travels had made him worldly and put him at ease with himself. He bore only a distant resemblance to that awkward boy Edie had first met in the winter of 1944.

All the hoopla jolted Edie into an exaggerated recognition of her first husband's fame. Like everyone else at the funeral, she was shocked when another of Jack's old poet friends, Gregory Corso, jumped down into the open grave at the Edson Cemetery to film the graveside services from the most appropriate angle. In addition to renewing her friendship with Allen, Edie found herself welcomed into the circle of the Sampas family. She told Stella of the letters (preserved, ironically, by Charlotte from the destructive wrath of their mother) she had from Jack and Gabrielle in the 1940s, and Stella encouraged her to publish them. Edie also met Tony Sampas, one of Stella's many brothers, who later wrote with advice about how to deal with Kerouac's first published biographer, Ann Charters.

These few glowering days in Lowell in October 1969 changed

Edie Parker at the Jack Kerouac Memorial
Monument in Lowell, MA, October 1988

Edie's life. Instead of the anonymous aging country-clubber living off the diminishing wealth of her mother's third husband, she became, once again, the wife of Jack Kerouac, and as Kerouac's fame grew in the years after his death, so did Edie's identification with the Beat period of her life. By the time she died of neglected diabetes in 1993, she had taken to using his last name again, forgotten that she had been married twice more in the interim, and even denied that their marriage had ever been annulled. At the last, as she struggled to put her memoirs, named for a phrase of reassurance in one of Jack's letters, into a publishable form, she had completely remade herself in order to vie with Carolyn Cassady as the queen of the Beat Generation. In these later years Edie rued the fact that no photos exist of her and Jack together.

The decade of the 1970s witnessed the beginnings of the cottage industry that has grown up around Kerouac. Ann Charters published her biography in 1973; it hasn't been out of print since. Others followed. The first academic conference on Kerouac's writing was held at Salem State University in 1974. In the late 1970s Gerald Nicosia began conducting interviews in preparation for his remarkably thorough biography, *Memory Babe*, thus preserving the voices of Edie Parker and many others who knew Kerouac personally. Gerry, as was his wont with many of those he interviewed, befriended Edie and served to some degree as her spokesman during these years. In 1982 Edie attended the Naropa Institute conference to celebrate the twenty-fifth anniversary of the publication of *On the Road*, a book with which she had little actual connection. On camera for a video production called *What Happened to Kerouac?* the still-exuberant first wife began to create her own version of her first husband, though at one point she had difficulty recalling just who it was the interviewer was asking her to recall.

The meeting in Boulder seems to have galvanized Edie's resolve to rewrite the record, because she devoted the rest of her life to gathering and synthesizing information about her past, especially the early 1940s. To that end she employed a series of secretaries, who often lived with her in a duplex she had inherited in a run-down part of Detroit. As Jim Perrizo's experience demonstrates, anyone who worked with Edie was sooner or later forced to deal with her unwillingness to separate fact from fantasy. Indeed, Edie often seemed unconcerned with the facts. What did it matter that records of both her civil and religious annulments still existed? Who cared if her own records failed to substantiate her claim that she had met Jack Kerouac soon after she came to New York and had lived with him steadily for five years? How could these young men, who were trying to help her tell her story, know better than she herself what she had experienced? For his efforts to ascertain the facts, Jim Perrizo was eventually replaced by another secretary, who would help Edie tell her story her own way or not at all.

F O U R

THE WOMAN WITHOUT
A BOURGEOIS BONE
IN HER BODY

She entered this world in Forest Hills, New York, the famous tennis venue, spent her childhood in Hollywood, came of age in a village south of Albany, married and raised four children in the slums of New York City after abandoning a brief experiment in conventional family life in the Midwest, went "back to the earth" in central Washington near the age of forty, and wound up the last decade of her life working as a neighborhood activist in Eugene, Oregon, while fighting a losing battle with breast cancer. Of all the dramatic lives that intersected with Jack Kerouac's, I find Joan Haverty's the most intriguing. Sometimes I wish I could have followed her during her strange odyssey, which I can only describe as a continuous, energetic attempt to escape from normalcy. Instead I have tracked her posthumously. As well as any fugitive from the American dream can be tracked, that is.

On Bell Avenue, a narrow, two-block street sandwiched between the railroad yards and an industrial spur in west Eugene, neighbors of Joan still remembered her lively storytelling five years after her death in 1990. And though part of the plum orchard at the west end of the street has been cut down, the small park Joan fought to wrest from the industrial sprawl is still filled with children on summer days. One man, himself a refugee from the East Coast, pointed out a flourishing apple tree that Joan had asked him to transplant from her yard just before she died. This same fellow recalled with great fondness Joan's storytelling abilities. She was the neighborhood celebrity, although her friend

Henry Jones, a former smoke jumper, probably held the title of neighborhood character.

Some of her friends had had a little college education sprinkled amid the hard work and hard times of their lives, so when Joan told them she had once been married to Jack Kerouac, the King of the Beatniks, they understood. Not awed, but appreciative. To them Jack Kerouac was only a name in the vast, glittering array of names known as celebrity. If the stories seemed somewhat overfinished, so what? Joan was a good person. As a community activist for VISTA — Volunteers in Service to America, a kind of domestic Peace Corps — she had won them a little park for their run-down neighborhood, she was fighting a brave fight against cancer, and she still found strength to regale her acquaintances with colorful anecdotes from her past. What did they care?

Some of these same neighbors also remember the frequent visits of Joan's daughters, Jan and Sharon, who still lives in Eugene. They knew her son, David, as a local musician, who lived on Bell Avenue with his mother and then returned briefly after his marriage. One recalled Jan as a "party girl," while still recognizing her devotion to her mother. Everyone had his or her favorite anecdote about Joan, but they all added up to the same thing: a good neighbor, a likable woman, and, in general, a fun person to be around.

It was Sharon Aly, Joan's daughter from her second marriage, who threw me the biggest curve as I was researching her mother's life. "Just remember," Sharon warned me in a phone conversation, "my mother was a liar. She preferred to tell it the way it should have been to the way it really was." Now what was I to do? How could I document the life of someone who didn't want her life to be objectively documented any more than necessary if I couldn't trust her own words? Worse yet, Sharon was reluctant to talk with me because of a warning from Jan, who had taken to referring to me as "that bastard." Talk she did, nevertheless, and thanks to her I was able to piece together the closing chapters in Joan Haverty's life.

I had gotten plenty of information from Jan, of course, while we were still on good terms, and I had had several phone conversations with Joan's only sibling, her brother Dave, a business executive in Atlanta. During a research trip to the Albany area in early summer 1995 I had also discovered a few documented facts about Joan and her mother, Violet Haverty. Violet is still alive as I write this, having recently celebrated her eighty-seventh birthday. She refused my repeated requests to speak with her, because, according to her son, she doesn't particularly care to contribute to the growing reputation of Jack Kerouac. In Violet's eyes, apparently, Jack Kerouac is still just the man who abruptly married her daughter, got her pregnant, then left her before the birth of their daughter. Jan herself never got along well with her stern Grandmother Haverty, and they exchanged only the most perfunctory correspondence. Violet never had much use for irresponsibility, I guess.

The most interesting source of information about Joan Haverty's life now appears — in light of Sharon's statement — to be the least reliable. It is her unpublished memoir, ironically titled *Nobody's Wife*. Her son David's brother-in-law has edited the mountain of handwritten notes, left by Joan under the bed in her little house in Eugene when she died, into a fascinating narrative of the year or so leading up to her marriage to Kerouac. Starting in the summer of 1949, it begins with a flashback to Joan's childhood, a recollection of her life with her grandparents in Hollywood during the Depression. According to Jan, her mother at the age of three had traveled by ocean liner from New York, where Joan was born in 1930, through the Panama Canal to California. What became of her father, John Haverty, or why he and Violet separated, remains a mystery to me. At any rate, Joan spent her childhood in movieland, returning to upstate New York with her mother and little brother in 1942 (Joan's memoir says 1943), according to a class history I found in the yearbook of Voorheesville High School, a rural consolidated school in the foothills of the Helderberg Mountains south of Albany.

Perhaps their move back to New York state had something to do with John Haverty's military career. He served as an officer in the South Pacific, and his son, Dave, recalls that he visited the family in their wood-shingled house at 7 Borthwich Avenue in Delmar, an Albany suburb. In any case, as the war effort went into high gear, while Violet worked in various Albany department

Joan Haverty, circa 1950

stores, Joan seems to have lived the normal life of a teenager of that period: saddle shoes and nicknames ("Scotty" to her best friend's "Bunny"), soda shops and school activities. Joan sang in the Voorheesville High School glee club, wrote for the student newspaper and yearbook, and acted in the senior play. During her senior year in school, 1947, she even served as secretary to the student council.

Like many of the girls in her graduating class, Joan looked older than her age. The caption under her senior yearbook photo describes her as a person with "sophistication, talent for acting," someone who was "musical, friendly and happy." Joan listed her own ambition as the wish to become an interior decorator, and with her best friend, Helen "Bunny" Brandon, she planned to attend the New York School of Interior Design. In the "Class Prophecy 1947" Helen predicted their future life as next-door neighbors in New Mexico, she on her "bunny farm" and Joan apparently still unmarried. But it was Joan's interest in theater, rather than her decorating skills, that led her to take her first step into adult life.

If Joan's account in *Nobody's Wife* can be trusted, in the two years after graduation her sophistication and model's good looks led her into theatrical circles in Albany. In the summer of 1949 an acquaintance in one of those circles, an older man she calls Cliff Pryat, suggested they spend a couple weeks in a resort in Provincetown. Apparently, Cliff's request, bold as it was, provided the necessary impetus for Joan to make her break from home. She accepted, and with little more than a suitcase and the clothes on her back, set out for Cape Cod with Cliff in his convertible.

Though she may have looked and acted sophisticated, Joan was still naive enough to misunderstand Cliff's motives. When they arrived in Provincetown, the theatrical hotel turned out to be nothing less than a sort of bohemian commune, and Joan soon discovered that Cliff expected her to share not only a ride, but a room and a bed as well. Without knowing where she would turn, Joan bolted, and to her credit she learned to survive on her own. This principled yet impulsive break from a man became the modus operandi, if not the theme, of her youth. Fate, however, soon put her on a path to New York City, where she would spend most of the next twenty years of her life.

Fate, in this instance, took the form of a handsome young lawyer named Bill Cannastra, a character well-known to readers of Beat lore as a notoriously self-destructive libertine. In *Nobody's Wife* Joan describes their initial encounter, her first bizarre attempts at sex with one of Bill's friends, and the beginning of their brief life together, Joan's introduction to la vie bohème. The bizarre character of their sexual liaison stemmed not only from the holiday atmosphere of Provincetown, but also from Bill's obvious bisexuality and Joan's strange tendency to depersonalize the act of intercourse. She describes her first attempts at lovemaking with Bill's buddy Steen with a startling lack of affect, a numbness from the waist down.

For his part, Bill seemed satisfied that his own relationship with Joan be primarily nonsexual. Some twisted Catholic rationale suggested to him that she would be better off "saving herself" for marriage, leaving him to pursue more diverse connections. Together they developed strange rituals to enliven the squalor of their minimal accommodations, like listening to Handel while the refrigerator leaked onto the living room floor. When the summer of 1949 drew to a close and Bill felt the tug of his law firm in New York, Joan faced the decision to return to her mother in rural Albany or to follow him down to the city. She chose life in a loft on West 21st Street.

For a little more than a year (Nicosia says two years), Joan shared a kind of life with Bill, trying to get a foothold in the city as he became increasingly maudlin and deranged. It seems impossible that during that year she could have failed to meet Jack Kerouac, a handsome, vibrant writer in Bill's circle of friends, especially since Bill's next-door neighbor was Lucien Carr, another Beat legend, and Allen Ginsberg had supposedly courted her in an attempt to suppress his homosexuality. But Joan's memoir substantiates the myth that she had never laid eyes on the blue-eyed ex-footballer until November 1950, two weeks before they were married. Despite her affinity for the stage, something in Joan's character made her withdraw from the wobbling center of Bill's bohemian life, and somewhere along the line she met a conventional young scientist named Herb Lashinsky. Perhaps in an attempt to retain some semblance of her mother's middle-class values in her new life, Joan became his lover.

Then came the night — October 12, 1950 — when Joan's first true lover, Bill Cannastra, passed forever from reality into legend. The event, described best in Alan Harrington's 1966 novel *The Secret Swinger*, went something like this. Cannastra, simulating devastation because of being rejected by his fiancée, went on a drinking spree with friends. At some point, they all went into the subway to catch a train uptown. After the gang had seated themselves, some remark made Bill decide to exit the train. In typical clownish fashion, he made as if to climb out a train window. Whether his friends prevented him from jumping safely to the platform, or whether he became wedged in the window, when the train left the platform, Bill's head struck a pillar and his body was pulled beneath the train. His gruesome death cast an existential pall over his entire circle of friends (similar to the result of the suicide in the film *Next Stop, Greenwich Village*), and Joan was so devastated when she heard the news that she immediately resolved to make Bill's loft into a shrine. No one recorded what Herb Lashinsky thought or felt about her resolution.

It seems odd, too, that Kerouac would not have known of Cannastra's death or of Joan's having taken possession of his apartment. He had heard of a party at Lucien's loft on the night of November 3. Wouldn't he have heard that Bill's friend Joan had taken the dead man's loft? She had heard of Jack from Bill long before his death. Wouldn't he have heard of her from the same source? Further, if he knew the party was at Lucien's, why did he call up to Cannastra's loft? Too many unanswered (and perhaps unanswerable) questions make Jack's meeting with Joan seem fated. As perhaps it was. Whatever the case, it was Herb Lashinsky who opened the loft door to his unknown rival, who entered flushed with the six-flight climb and the anticipation of a week-end of partying.

Fresh from his first trip to Mexico (the same one with Neal Cassady he fictionalized in *On the Road*) and now in the throes of writing a book to follow up the recent publication of his first novel, *The Town and the City*, Kerouac at age twenty-eight had become obsessed with the need to marry. His first attempt in 1944, had, in fact, been a marriage of convenience prompted by his friend Lucien's run-in with the law. Though he was perhaps as far from being trapped as he would ever be in his life in 1950, Jack now began to act in a similarly desperate manner. The very first words out of his mouth as he entered Cannastra's loft were, according to Joan's memoir, to ask Herb whether she was his girl.

When Herb said no, it was almost as if he had told Jack, "Go ahead, you can marry her."

Something about Joan's appearance — she was wearing a skirt because all her dungarees were dirty — and her activity — she was making hot chocolate — caused Jack to misperceive her true nature. And once he got it into his head that she was a homebody, comfortable with domestic chores, he immediately determined to make her his wife. The next night he returned to propose, and for reasons Joan could not even explain to herself, she accepted. On November 17, exactly two weeks after they met (according to the myth), Joan and Jack were married by one of his cousins who was a New York judge. Their life together lasted all of six months.

Ordinarily, marriage heralds the convergence of lives, and as 1950 merged into 1951, Jack and Joan experienced briefly the beginnings of the melding of two families by means of the creation of a third. Dave Haverty recalls visits to Albany made by the newlyweds, one prompted by a book-signing party for *The Town and the City* sponsored by Violet's department store. One evening he and his buddies, who had only graduated from high school the previous spring, took Jack drinking in the roadhouses in the Helderberg Mountains. On another occasion Jack and Joan brought one of Jack's literary pals along, although years later Allen Ginsberg could not remember making the trip upstate. Another thing Dave recalled that seems to have been omitted from the record of Kerouac's life is a wedding reception thrown by Joan's father in Washington, DC, where he had moved after the war and gone into the billboard business. It was a lavish affair, Dave recalls, to which only the Haverty side of the family was invited.

Jack planned to relocate to the West Coast, so he and Joan could be near Neal and Carolyn. To economize, the young couple moved in with Jack's mother in Richmond Hill just before Christmas, but this cozy arrangement lasted less than a month, before Joan, who was still only twenty years old, realized she was being turned into a child again by yet another mother. For his part, Jack reported their troubles in a long letter to Neal, in which he confessed he was "torturing" his new wife in some way. One day in January 1951 she had her things moved while Jack's mother was at work. Joan instructed the movers that Jack could come along if he wanted. When she came to her new place on West 20th Street during her lunch break to check on their progress, she found him waiting on the sidewalk. In February, however, Kerouac complained to the eminent man of letters Alfred Kazin that he was trapped in an American tragedy.

In terms of breakthroughs in writing, 1951 was Jack Kerouac's annus mirabilis. Tutored by his buddy Neal Cassady's torrential letters and inspired by the sketching of another Denver pal, Ed White, Jack quickly discovered the method of composition he came to call "spontaneous prose." No wonder he became increasingly oblivious to Joan's growing discontent. She resented being excluded from his adventures with his male friends — a kind of treatment Bill had never subjected her to — and she simply refused to wait on him the way his mother did. He was almost twenty-nine, for Pete's sake.

Then, in early April, shortly after Jack's birthday, a strange thing happened. He sat down at his typewriter and didn't get up for three weeks, except to sleep and relieve himself. He screwed the butt-end of a teletype paper roll, salvaged for him by Lucien Carr from the UPI office, hung it onto a coat hanger over his typewriter, and began to blast out a hundred-foot-long version of his new book at 100 WPM. Joan fed him coffee and pea soup. Jack sweated and lost weight. It was the big game, and he was playing his heart out.

Sometime during Jack's marathon, or perhaps shortly after he finished it, he did something he rarely did: he made love to his wife. Joan liked to imagine that it happened while he was writing "the Mexican girl" episode of On the Road, because she believed that Jack could only get sexual with a woman if he felt he was her social or intellectual superior. Timing suggests that it probably happened in May, however, after Jack had already finished the scroll manuscript and their marriage had fallen apart, not least because of the intensity of his new writing method.

As fate would have it, however, Joan became pregnant. Though Jack afterward recalled the presence of a Puerto Rican busboy in his wife's boudoir — and Lord knows, anything is possible in such bohemian circumstances — one look at his grown daughter was

enough to convince most people that Jan was the genuine article, a chip off the old Kerouac block. But perhaps to prevent his
mother from forcing him to reconcile with Joan for the sake of
the coming baby, Jack kept silent about her pregnancy and later
publicly denied that he had fathered a child. Sometime that
spring, the couple split up. Jack wrote to his buddy Neal on June
10, 1951, that Joan had already moved back upstate and that he
was leaving their apartment the next day.

I hesitate to say who left whom, because such technicalities are
often magnified into decisive details under the law (and there is
something to be said for this), but it was Joan's idea to move out
of Gabrielle's apartment, and Jack recorded in his diary that he
had been "thrown out" by his wife after their first reconciliation.
Not much evidence exists to suggest that either one of them
really took their wedding vows very seriously. While Joan seems
to have been understandably preoccupied in the following years
with making Jack live up to his legal responsibility to support his
child (which he failed to do even minimally until forced into court
nearly a decade later), letters from the late 1960s indicate that
she felt little personal rancor toward him, and it seems likely
that she was relieved to be rid of such a big baby when she had
a little one on the way.

Whatever the case, this couple, who had barely become ac-
quainted with each other, now parted ways. Neither one bothered
to file for divorce. From its whirlwind beginning their marriage
seemed more of a scene that he had written and she had acted,
and Jack showed no more concern for it than he had when he left
his first marriage. In her actions, Joan cast the mold for her subsequent repeated flights from stability and respectability in marriage.
And so began, contrary to convention, a fable of divergence.

Probably against her better judgment, Joan retreated to her
mother's home outside Albany for the last stage of her pregnancy. From this distance she filed a complaint against Jack for
nonsupport, and he was jailed briefly after being discharged
from the VA hospital in late summer. The new year brought no
overtures of reconciliation from either party. On February 16,
1952, Janet Michele Kerouac was born. At about the same time,
however, Joan's grandfather fell ill in California, and Violet was

called to the West Coast to assist her parents. Brother Dave came to the rescue instead. After closing up the house in Delmar and putting their mother's belongings in storage, brother and sister and baby Jan became a family, living together for several years while following Dave's good job with the telephone company. One of Jan's earliest memories was of their home in Binghamton: "Unkie Day," as she called him, passing her crib late one night after going out with some of his buddies from the army reserve. Sometime during this period Joan spent a few months in the old-fashioned Oneonta TB sanatorium in upstate New York. She continued to use the law to force Jack to live up to his parental responsibilities, but his initial bitterness following their breakup seems to have faded within a few years.

Photos from these years show Jan as a quite normal fifties child, wearing bobby socks and riding a tricycle around her uncle's new Chevy. In 1956 Violet returned from California to settle in Wappingers Falls outside Poughkeepsie. Joan and Jan stayed with her briefly after Dave was called to active duty in Germany, but living with her mother apparently inspired Joan to return to the city to try once again to make it on her own. On a day trip she found a cheap apartment and a waitressing job, and soon she and Jan began their life together in the city. But fate intervened once more, and their time alone proved to be short. This time fate took the form of a fresh-faced Midwesterner who had come to New York to become a painter.

Bower John Aly was the same age as Joan, and his background was probably more similar to hers than was Jack's. In fact, his stable roots and provincial ways probably both attracted and repelled Joan, as they reflected her own paradoxical desires. Whatever the reasons, one day, after dropping the baby off at the sitter, Joan came to her job in a restaurant/gallery to find a young painter hanging his work. He asked her name, they began to talk, and the rest, as they say, is history. Soon Joan was pregnant again, but this time without benefit of marriage.

About the time Joan and Jack split up, John Aly had his first exhibition as part of the renowned Art Students' League. He had dropped out of the University of Missouri, where his father was an eminent member of the faculty, to follow his dream in the city.

Joan Haverty and Jan Kerouac on
Park Avenue, New York, circa 1955

His father and stepmother were duly horrified, but perhaps not
as much as when, six years later, he announced that he was about
to marry a woman who was not only pregnant, but possessed of
a four-year-old daughter by a man to whom she was still married.
Thinking he was doing the right thing by abandoning his ambition to become an artist and returning to college, he begged his
parents to let them have the basement apartment in their big new
house on Westmount Drive in Columbia until they could get on
their feet. He would finish his degree, then get a job teaching art
in the public schools.

Four or five months pregnant, Joan set off alone on the bus for
Juarez, the nearest place where she could obtain a Mexican
divorce. In a bar near her cheap accommodations there, one of
the patrons teased her in Spanish that she was obviously a
woman with a past. Divorce in hand, she returned to Missouri in
June to marry John. In November, while her first husband was
suffering the initial torments of celebrity following the publication of *On the Road*, she gave birth to twin girls, Kathy and
Sharon, in New York City Hospital. When they were old enough

to travel, mother and daughters left the city for the country, and in the 1950s, Columbia, Missouri, though world-famous for its school of journalism, was still deep, deep in the country.

Jan's recollection of their move was distinct and vivid. She was a city girl by nature, and after just a few months of life on the Lower East Side, with all its activity and diversity, the prospect of growing up on a quiet, tree-lined street in small-town Missouri dismayed her. Perhaps her loathing for her new life (probably a reflection of her mother's less obvious reaction) colored her recollection of the family circumstances. In her first novel, *Baby Driver*, and in interviews, Jan painted a picture of the conservative Aly family, embarrassed by the return of the prodigal son with (probably) profligate wife in tow. Jan believed they were installed in the basement to hide the family's shame, though my guess is that it was a simple convenience born of family feeling. Even prestigious professors like the elder Bower Aly made little money in the 1950s, and the basement apartment provided the family a way to live in style without breaking the bank. Support for this supposition lies in the fact that when the elder Aly left Columbia to start the communications department at the University of Oregon, he installed his son's family in a small house on Aldeah Street, probably his first home in Columbia, which he had retained as a rental property. In any case, Jan despised Midwestern life, recalling in her fictionalized autobiography that the most exciting thing that happened during their stay in Missouri was that a tornado blew the roof off a neighbor's house one summer.

Perhaps the eldest daughter also sensed something lacking in her mother's relationship with her stepfather. Certainly, her account of their life together in *Baby Driver* suggests more antagonism than love, and perhaps Jan, with a child's intuition, perceived that her mother had married this man out of convenience, as a way to provide for her growing family and escape from the degradation of their worsening poverty in the city. Be that as it may, John Aly apparently did what he could to put a good face on the situation. He went back to college to finish his art degree. While he studied, Joan played at being the conventional housewife and mother. Some pundit in San Francisco had now named the rebellious members of her generation in imitation of the first

Russian satellite, Sputnik, and occasionally, her days were brightened by letters from Jack, who was now being hyped by the media as "King of the Beatniks." Ed Sanders, a younger Beat poet, an undergraduate at Mizzou in those years, recalls that after *On the Road* was published, someone he knew gained access to Joan's letters from Jack, and they were passed around the circle of students who had read and admired his novel.

In the summer of 1958 John landed a job teaching art in Trenton, an even smaller town in the Amish hill country of northwestern Missouri. This was probably the last straw for Joan, who may have been able to tolerate life in a university town slightly better than in an arch-conservative bastion like Trenton. Jan was already attending third grade in the old brick school on Main Street that now houses the junior college. The twins had grown into toddlers, and probably the combination of boredom, revolt from the uniformity of small-town life, missing the excitement of the city, and the better mobility of slightly older children combined to prompt Joan to escape. Jan's recollection of the event places the blame squarely and simply on John Aly's shoulders: he went away somewhere without leaving Joan enough money to run the household. Possible, but I suspect this is a prejudiced child's oversimplification. The fact remains, Joan put herself and her daughters on a train and took them on the two-day journey back to New York City. Her sojourn in the Midwest marked her last attempt to live any semblance of a middle-class life.

As the 1950s drew to a close, Joan must have realized more fully the dangers of the trap she had fallen into. Despite cheaper rents, the welfare mother's situation was the same then as it is now: a vicious cycle. Low-wage jobs provided too little income to pay for child care. Joan was forced to improvise. She moved from one cheap flat to another, then into condemned buildings. Rarely was there any hot water, never a phone. Jan learned too, using her girlish good looks to distract shop owners when she shoplifted. Even at this early age — she was now approaching eight — she acquired a taste for gourmet food, and she often pocketed expensive jars of jam instead of staples. Sometimes, however, her mother's neighborhood connections netted the family provisions from a pilfered delivery truck. By hook or by crook, they got by.

Some of Jack Kerouac's letters from the mid- to late 1950s reveal an unflattering side of his character: he was on the lam from his ex-wife. He adopted an absurd alias and instructed his friends to address letters to him under his assumed name. His frequent trips to Mexico, which ended abruptly at the end of the decade, may be explained in part by his attempts to elude the not-so-long arm of the child enforcement division of the New York district attorney's office.

Joan was persistent, however, and as her desperation increased, so did her demands that Jack face up to his financial responsibility to Jan. He did so reluctantly, melodramatically, grumbling all the way to his paternity hearing in January 1961. Represented in court by Allen Ginsberg's lawyer brother, Jack submitted to a blood test that proved that at the very least he *could* have been Jan's father. Later, he submitted to the judge's ruling that he pay a measly $52 a month child support, reduced to the minimum because of Jack's plea that he was still afflicted by phlebitis. Afterward, Jack and Joan and Jan went to lunch in Brooklyn, and then mother and daughter took him back to their apartment. It was the first time Jan had ever laid eyes on her father. Another technicality that was obscured by later media coverage of Jan: legally, Jack was declared to be her father in 1961.

Finally, Joan could count on at least a pittance from Jack, and John, presumably, willingly helped support his own daughters, although for some reason Joan refused to allow him to see them for almost seven years. To make a bit of extra money she sold the story of the paternity suit to *Confidential* magazine, and one of the New York tabloids picked up the news from the court records. About this time she also met another man, a wacky ne'er-do-well named Harry Peace. Harry and his black friends amused Jan no end, and despite his heavy drinking, Joan stayed with him long enough to become pregnant, although she apparently later denied that Harry had fathered her fourth child. In Washington State, in fact, she sometimes pretended that David was an orphan she had taken in out of kindness. Now she had four mouths to feed on her public-aid check. Things were not getting any easier.

Throughout the 1960s the pressures on Joan mounted. John Aly pressed her for visitation rights to Sharon and Kathy. And at age twelve, with no moral guidance from her mother, Jan discovered the new staple of street life — drugs. She smoked pot, started sleeping with boys, some of them much older than herself, and became defiant. Joan enrolled herself and Jan in a program for troubled teens at Bellevue. At wit's end, she finally had Jan committed. It hurt more than it helped, and Jan rebelled by getting in trouble with the law. Joan's brother, now married, came down to take Jan back to Duchess County with him. She lasted a couple weeks, then frightened Dave's wife and kids so much that he was forced to take her back to the city. Jan promptly moved in with a drug pusher who lived down the hall. The last straw: at age fifteen Jan herself got pregnant.

The mounting pressure must have got to Joan, because just before Thanksgiving 1967, she agreed to allow John Aly to see his daughters for the first time since their mother had taken them from Missouri. Though I can't be sure, I think John's parents may have suggested the course of action that followed. Suspecting that Joan was not a fit mother — a reasonable suspicion viewed from afar — they probably offered their son the money to send the twins to Oregon, which he did.

At the same time, Jan talked her new boyfriend, a serious and intelligent young man from Maine named John Lash, into taking her to Mexico. Before they left, however, they would take the bus up to Lowell to see her father. Perhaps he would give them some money. In any case, Jan had talked to him on the phone at least once, and she wanted to see him again before she left the country. Suddenly, Joan had only her son David left to care for, but she was determined to follow and find her twin daughters, to expose their father's act of kidnapping, and to regain custody. In a matter of months, after she scraped together enough money for a bus ticket to the West Coast, she abandoned the squalor of her life in New York City for squalor of a new kind.

Instead of proceeding directly to Eugene, however, Joan took David to San Francisco, where she found a cheap apartment in Hayes Valley, near the foot of Haight Street. Perhaps she half intended to follow Jan to Mexico to be with her during the birth of her child. Perhaps she felt more comfortable in a larger town. In any event she waxed philosophical in letters to Jack, wondering as he often did whether parenthood was such a good idea after all. When she finally got to Oregon, after a detour through Seattle, the court had already awarded custody of the children to the elder Alys, and the twins had been separated, Sharon staying with her grandparents in Eugene and Kathy being sent up to Ellensburg, Washington, to live with an aunt and uncle. For some reason, Joan followed Kathy, and when Jan returned from Mexico, childless, via more than a year in San Francisco, where she and John were married, she found her mother ensconced in a tiny little house in the tiny little town of Kittitas, just a few miles east of Ellensburg, in central Washington. Just as Joan was settling in, Jack Kerouac died of alcoholism in Florida. Jan heard the news on her way up the coast.

In the rugged surroundings of the far West, nearing the age of forty, Joan found expression for her many eccentricities. Amid the brown treeless hills of the Kittitas Valley, with the snowcapped peaks of the Cascades in the background to the northwest, she finally let it all hang out. She chopped her own wood, heated coffee on the stove incessantly, and ripped out the insulation from the walls, so that the winter wind whistled right through. She botched the reinstallation of the toilet, so that both she and little David had to go into the backyard to squat. She was crazy, it appears, but she was also free, and gradually some direction came back into her life. When summer came she began to garden furiously, putting in a huge strawberry bed. Recalling the piece she had done for *Confidential* a decade ago, she thought of becoming a freelance writer. Eventually, she moved into Ellensburg and tried to get a job with a local community service agency.

Jan often came to stay with her mother in Washington State. She recalled fondly the times with her brother David in an upstairs apartment on Ruby Street, next to a supermarket just north of downtown Ellensburg. Like Joan in her younger days, she took to doing restaurant work, and even went to college for a couple semesters, sharing her love of the Spanish language with her mother as well. Sometimes Joan saw her younger daughter, Kathy, on the streets with her friends, but they never spoke. Apparently, Joan feared that Kathy had been poisoned against her by her in-laws. Rather than find out for sure, she asked Jan to relay messages to her half-sister. It was a weird scene, no doubt, but it suited them, and they lived more or less happily.

In 1974, when Kathy returned to do her senior year in high school in Eugene (she wanted to establish residency so she could go to the university there), Joan lost focus again. She began to fantasize about her Scottish heritage and even planned to emigrate to Scotland. Though she never acted on her plan, as a result of it, after consulting David, she changed their name to Stuart. And somehow, after all those years, she hooked up with her old boyfriend, Herb Lashinsky. According to Jan, their renewed relationship marked the "last fling" of Joan's life.

Around 1980 she moved with David to Eugene, where she found another little house in a secluded neighborhood. Now she was near both twins, and David seemed to thrive in the new environment. He was a tinkerer, and like many of his contemporaries, he loved to play guitar. In Eugene he eventually gained a modest reputation as a singer-songwriter. His mother took to her new neighborhood, making friends and getting involved in community efforts to improve the living conditions just west of the railyards. She was taken up as a kind of folk hero by the local lesbian community. Eventually, she became a VISTA volunteer, continuing her community organizing with a modest stipend from the government.

Then in 1982, tragedy struck. Joan was diagnosed with breast cancer. Having no insurance and no money for treatment, she fought the disease as best she could with home remedies. According to her family and friends, she never lost her spirit, and for a time the cancer went into remission. When it returned, however, it returned with a vengeance. Joan underwent a double mastectomy. By the last year of her life, she looked more like a skeleton than a live woman. Always proud of her personal appearance, she shunned help from her family, preferring the services of a hired woman. Still, she continued to be neighborly, treating all comers to tales of Kerouac and her glory days in New York. In the summer of 1989 there was a kind of family reunion. Kathy came home from Cyprus, where she had gone to teach English, married a Greek man, and settled down to raise a family. Dave Haverty flew in from Atlanta. Jan had been living in Eugene for a few years and had begun to have health problems of her own. But at least they were all together.

Despite their fears for Joan's survival, the daughters were unable to express their love for their mother adequately. Heart-to-heart talks were brushed aside in favor of more lighthearted feelings, but Sharon recalls that at one moment Joan did remark on the similarities between her personality and Jan's. "There was no middle ground for either of them," Sharon told me. "Like Mom, with Jan you're either a sheep or a goat." Sharon does not consider her mother's life in any way admirable: "She could *seem* admirable, like she had made a lot out of a little rather than a little out of a lot." The one conviction Sharon retains today that she learned from her mother's bad example: not to lie.

Though her health actually improved for a while after seeing the family all together, Joan Virginia Haverty Stuart died in Sacred Heart Hospital in Eugene on Mother's Day, May 15, 1990. Coincidentally, her second husband, John Aly, whom his daughter Sharon describes as "a pitiful alcoholic," died in Seattle less than two months later. Later that same year, Jack Kerouac's third wife, Stella Sampas, also died. It was a year of death for these disconnected families, and soon Jan would have serious health problems of her own. Joan's last request was that her ashes be planted with a Tropicana rose bush the next time her children all gathered together. So far that has yet to happen, and as of August 1995, Joan's ashes rested on a bookshelf in Sharon Aly's home in Eugene, a home she bought with a bequest from her father's stepmother, who also died in 1990.

FIVE

A BLOCK OFF THE OLD CHIP

After a relatively pleasant early childhood with her Uncle Dave acting as surrogate father, Jan returned with her mother to New York City, as I say, where they lived in a series of cheap flats, mostly on the Lower East Side. Just as Jan was learning to dig the street life, her stepfather, John Aly, dragged the family off to Columbia, Missouri, where he had grown up. At first, they lived in the basement of his father's house, a virtual mansion on the west side of town. Bower Aly, a distinguished professor of debate at the University of Missouri, was in the process of changing jobs, having taken up the task of founding the speech department at the University of Oregon, so John, Joan, Jan, and the babies soon moved into the little house on Aldeah Street where John had grown up.

Jan later recalled the move to the hinterlands as a dreadful bore. As she searched up and down the long, narrow, tree-lined street of bungalows, she missed the noise and excitement of her old neighborhood in the city. She pointedly looked down on her playmates, spent a good deal of time at the nearby public library, and relished the infrequent moments of Midwestern excitement, such as the summer day a tornado struck nearby, detaching the neighbors' porch roof and twirling it into a vacant lot. But as far as she could tell, they were here to stay. Now that he had a family to support, John Aly thought it proper to abandon his bohemian lifestyle, return to college for his art degree, and take up a stable, if unlucrative, career as an art teacher. After two years in Columbia, he landed a job as head of the art program in the Trenton, Missouri, school district.

If Jan thought Columbia was boring, she had another think coming, as they say up in the hilly Amish country of northwest

Missouri. Jan soon found herself in what might as well have been an outpost on the frontier. For compensation, she enjoyed the big house John was able to rent just behind Main Street (not exactly the Sinclair Lewis version, but close), near Five Points and the historic Episcopalian church. The Negro hospital was just a couple blocks to the north, on Jan's way to Trenton's rather large central grade school, where she was enrolled in third grade. Joan tried to help her fit in by signing her up for the Brownies. As the sights and sounds of the Lower East Side faded from the child's memory, she reverted to the happy acceptance of life on the terms it was given to her, just as she had when she and Mommy lived with "Unkie Day" in upstate New York.

Then, suddenly, one summer day, when her stepfather was out of town on school business, Jan came home to find boxes stacked in the hallway. As she stood musing on the almost certain meaning of this scene, a cricket chirped under one of the boxes, investing the memory with its sign of good luck. The next day Jan found herself seated on an eastbound railroad train, partly in charge of watching the toddling twins. After the complacent lull of three years in Missouri, Joan had had enough of small-town life and family values. She, too, longed for the excitement of the city, or at least for an escape from the tedium of the prospect of spending the rest of her life in Trenton. To an outsider's eyes, the four females looked like a happy family en route to visit relatives back East, and when they checked into an uptown hotel, the frilly dresses and the Midwestern address satisfied the management that Joan's credit was good. It took them a month to figure out that it wasn't, and by that time Joan had located a cheap apartment. The girls were so engrossed in the adventure of their flight that they scarcely noticed the shift from bourgeois life to splendor to poverty. They had their own little home again, and Jan, for her part, was anxious to rediscover the sidewalks of New York.

But her mother was hard up for money, and since she had technically deserted her husband, she couldn't very well make a claim on him. She could, however, make a claim on Jack Kerouac, who hadn't contributed a penny to Jan's keep since she was in the womb in late 1951. Now that Joan was on her own again, and

Jan was almost nine, it was high time to dun Jack for child support. Fearful perhaps that he would eventually be forced to pay, or worse, that he might have to acknowledge Jan as his child and shoulder some responsibility for her rearing, Kerouac spent most of the early 1950s on the road between New York, San Francisco, and Mexico City, at times using his mother's family name as a ruse to prevent Joan from locating him. She had gotten him into court once, in January 1954, but the judge had taken pity on Jack's condition — he was suffering a bout of his recurrent phlebitis at the time — and let him off the hook.

This is the period in which he wrote many of his novels, including the one that made him instantly famous, *On the Road*. Though it got hung up in the editorial process for a couple years, when it finally appeared in September 1957, Jack could no longer find a place to hide, nor could he pretend to be indigent and dependent on his mother for support. To the world's eyes, not to mention Joan's, he looked every bit like a successful novelist. A few years later Joan exploited this discrepancy by writing a true-confessions-style article for *Confidential* magazine. But for the moment Jack was at least visible. In 1961 he was ordered by the court to submit to a blood test, so that his type could be compared to Jan's to determine the probability of his paternity.

As the law would have it, both Jack and Jan were scheduled to appear on the same day in January 1961 for their tests, and since it now seemed inevitable that he would be forced to recognize the existence of his daughter, Jack behaved with as much good grace as he could muster. With his lawyer, Allen Ginsberg's brother Eugene Brooks, Jack walked down Flatbush Avenue in Brooklyn with his ex-wife and daughter, whom he had never seen till that day. Jan spotted a bar sign that advertised food — she spelled out B-A-R to impress her dad (though this story of hers sounds mingled with earlier childhood fantasy) — and they all stopped for a sandwich.

After lunch, Brooks went his way, and Jack passed out in the cab as he accompanied Joan and Jan back to their apartment, where he met the twins. Sharon recalled years later the funny man who had made a prediction that stuck in her mind: she would be the smart one, while her sister Kathy would be the pretty one. Jan herself drew the happy assignment of leading her father, already a serious alcoholic, to the neighborhood liquor store, where for some reason he bought a bottle of Harvey's Bristol Cream. When I met Jan in 1995, over thirty years after this first meeting with her dad, she still kept a bottle of Harvey's out on her kitchen counter as a kind of shrine to the memory of a pleasant afternoon with a funny drunk she showed off to her playmates as ''my father,'' in case they didn't believe she really had one. After a long chat, during which Jack spoke in a goofy Russian accent, the father she had never known wandered off where he had come from, bound this time for oblivion. Jan didn't see him again for six years. In the meantime, her mother bore another child, David, who became Jan's favorite sibling.

By the time Jan was nine she had already gotten her period, and though she didn't really enjoy sex until she was nearly forty, she discovered the pleasures of boys and drugs at about the same time. Like her father, Jan never did anything halfway. Whatever it

Jan's shrine to her father and mother, with
sherry bottle and her mother's favorite perfume

was, she went for it. When she was twelve or thirteen she lost her virginity to a black boy from her neighborhood. Pretty soon she started keeping score. By the time she was fourteen, Jan told me, she had had sex with a hundred boys. Most of these were brief encounters, but Jan thought she was really in love at age thirteen with Paul Ortloff, a twenty-year-old student at Cooper Union and erstwhile tattoo artist. As a sign of her devotion, she accepted the gift of a small black star, which he etched on her hip.

The sixties were just coming on, and Paul and Jan got high a lot. For her birthday in 1965 Paul sent her a card with a garland of joints inside. Seeing Jan getting stoned all the time with a much older guy naturally caused Jan's mother some anxiety, and the two began to quarrel. Joan was worried that Jan's drug abuse would spoil her chances to get a good education. Just a year before, Jan had tested into Hunter College Junior High School, where she suddenly found herself surrounded by fairly well-to-do kids who appreciated the finer things in life. Because she was intelligent as well as streetwise, Jan enjoyed the rigorous human-istic education at Hunter. Her long-standing interest in languages may have begun here, because decades later she still told stories about her Latin teacher. But she was living in two worlds: one of sophisticated children already marked for careers, the other of dropouts from careers.

Jan did most of her homework on the way to and from school, and afterward she hung with Paul or in good weather engaged in her favorite pastime of climbing to the roof of her building with a Hostess cherry pie to look out over the rooftops to the East River. She also got some cheap thrills by shoplifting, but her petty crime — which she still practiced just a year or so before her death — took an interesting twist. Instead of ripping off the obvi-ous stuff like books or records, Jan went for expensive gourmet food. Scottish marmalade, imported tea, that sort of thing. What shopkeeper would suspect this innocent-looking, black-haired, blue-eyed girl of filling her purse with jars of fancy condiments? When I went to visit Jan in Albuquerque in 1995, her kitchen table was still full of such items, though as far as I could tell, she never ate any of the stuff — Lapham Tangerine Marmalade, Dundee Morello Cherry Preserves, Cary's Maple Syrup — now purchased with royalties from Jack Kerouac's novels rather than with the five-finger discount. No, by this time Jan was into snatching vintage clothes at the local resale shops. Even after kidney failure, a girl can still use an occasional thrill.

During one of her sexual escapades Jan crossed paths with her father's old buddy Henri Cru. Jan was having an affair with a middle-aged Japanese man who lived in the same building as Cru, and when Henri realized what was going on, he began to refer to Jan as Lolita and offered to buy her some sexy underwear. In the afternoons Jan and her friends discovered that if they waited till the usher at the neighborhood art theater started to clean the restrooms, they could sneak into the matinee. In this way Jan saw many of the classic European films, such as *Black Orpheus*. Like some of the other kids, Jan also got interested in the street theater that Raul Julia had begun to organize on the Lower East Side. Years later Jan recalled performing with many of her neighbors in a play that featured a burning mattress being thrown from the top of a building onto the set. A stage fight turned real because two of the boys fell out of their roles while they were grappling and started to try to hurt each other. Jan was so impressed by the entire spectacle that she began to idolize Julia.

Joan tried sending Jan to live with Uncle Dave, who had married and settled in Duchess County to start a family. He and his wife already had two children. Jan dutifully packed up her clothes and other necessaries, and she didn't forget to bring along Paul's birthday gift, either. Needless to say, Dave found Jan incorrigible. Foul language and street smarts he may have been able to tolerate, but the presence of a budding pothead was too much. He shipped her back to the city with no apologies to Joan. Yet years later, this sane, stable man was still willing to help Jan, but naturally she never called on him for advice, preferring always the abusive, alcoholic, incompetent man. Like her mother, Jan seemed to have an aversion to middle-class values, and she often avoided them by attaching herself to a man who made sure she stayed in his downward spiral. What I find oddly admirable in this self-destructive behavior is clarity of vision coupled with an undeniable strength of will, both at the service of her sense of adventure and desire for freedom.

Back in New York City, Jan quickly precipitated a crisis by smoking up what was left of her pot and working herself into hysterics when her mother insisted that she stop seeing Paul for good. Already at thirteen Jan was incredibly headstrong. She threw such a tantrum that Joan, hoping to jolt her back into reality, phoned Bellevue, where they had been participating in a series of parent-teenager workshops. When the men in white suits arrived at the apartment door, Jan totally lost it. When they asked her to get her things ready to go to the hospital, she pulled out her jewelry drawer and poured the contents into her over-night bag. By this time, she was hallucinating, probably more from her own excitement than from the marijuana. But the men in white suits were taking no chances. These young ones could fool you. No sense risking getting hurt. With only a glance exchanged between them for warning, the two burly attendants sprang on Jan and wrestled her to the bed. They hog-tied her in a straitjacket as Joan looked on in utter astonishment and horror. Then they whisked Jan into a waiting van and took her to the hospital.

Before Joan could collect her wits and get ahold of their case-worker, Jan made a serious blunder. She told the admitting psychiatrist that she wanted to kill herself. After a hasty con-ference with colleagues, the doctor ordered Jan committed to the juvenile ward. He declared her dangerous to herself, and after that, there was nothing Joan could do to get her out. Jan describes her weeks in the psych ward at Bellevue in *Baby Driver*. She was harassed by both staff and inmates, threatened and intimidated, bullied and beaten, until she made friends with the toughest of the girls by drawing ink tattoos on their arms and legs. After that, Jan achieved a lowly status that at least kept her safe. But still she had to watch the daily assaults on other weak girls, and the bestiality of hospital life sickened her. Something about her time in Bellevue changed Jan. Instead of being chas-tened and scared, as her mother had hoped, Jan graduated into juvenile delinquency.

When the hospital administration was finally persuaded to release Jan, Joan reluctantly made a pact with her daughter: since Jan was clearly going to do as she wished, and since Joan was obviously unable to prevent her from doing as she wished, the mother declared her parental responsibility at an end. She would continue to love Jan and provide a home of sorts for her, but in the future she would place no restrictions on her behavior. In return, Joan would accept no blame or responsibility for the outcome of any of Jan's actions. In effect, Jan was declared an adult at an age when most adolescents still have one foot in childhood. I don't think Jan saw much danger in this premature freedom; she hit the street running. Her only complaint in adulthood was that even though her mother had a moral code of her own, she was incapable or unwilling to instill a similar code into her daughter. Consequently, Jan was left without a sense of what was good and bad in the long run.

Paul soon broke off their relationship, although he always kept in touch with her in later years, after he moved to an artists' community upstate. Jan bounced around from boy to boy for another year or so before landing in the arms of a Puerto Rican neighbor who sold drugs out of his apartment down the hall from her mother's place. Michael Duarte respected his new girlfriend's intelligence and her willingness to learn Spanish, and his chaotic lifestyle allowed Jan the freedom to do as she pleased most of the time, as long as she pleased him when he wanted to be pleased. And money was plentiful. At fifteen, Jan had already ascended to hippie heaven, and her mother was living right down the hall, no less. Jan let her hair grow long, almost down to her waist, and most of Michael's friends and clients took her for Hispanic.

And then, the worm in the apple: Jan got pregnant, as it turned out, for the first of eight times in her life. Wanting to keep the baby and sensing that Michael would not grow into a responsible father in the foreseeable future, Jan found herself in a dilemma. Several run-ins with the law after her stay in Bellevue had landed her briefly in the Bronx Reformatory. She now had a record, and she was on probation. Pregnancy was considered a violation of probation, and if Jan reported her condition to the probation officer, the state would probably throw her in a prison hospital until she delivered, then put the baby up for adoption, and send Jan to jail. Or so she believed, in any case.

Enter John Lamb Lash, one of the few stable elements in Jan's existence, and the love of her life, star English major from the University of Maine at Orono (where he shared that distinction with an unknown writer named Stephen King), fresh from a spiritual junket to India. As luck would have it, Lash moved in on the same floor as Jan and Joan and Michael. Spotting this good-looking older boy (he was all of twenty-one), Jan trumped up a reason to knock on his door. Her mother needed to borrow a can-opener. Did he have one? Certainly, and she was welcome to it. After finding out his name (which, ironically, was the same as her father's), Jan inquired about all the Indian artifacts and browsed through his books. One thing led to another, as they say, and pretty soon Jan was making daily detours into John's flat on her way from Michael's to her mother's.

A readily available John began to substitute for a missing Jack. Pretty soon John became number 48 (it should have been far higher, by my reckoning), as Jan recorded in her journal, though naturally she never told him his rank. She felt about John as she felt about no one else except her mother, and Jan considered him as much a soul-mate as Joan. Apparently, the feeling was mutual, and of course, with his literary background John knew the identity of Jan's errant father. In fact, Jan told him that Allen Ginsberg and his lover, Peter Orlovsky, had stopped her on the street in the Village one day to encourage her to get in touch with Jack. They gave her his phone number in Lowell, where he was again living, now with his third wife, Stella, a hometown girl. Jan told John that she had phoned Jack once, and they had a pleasant enough chat about their common French ancestry, but nothing more came of it.

Jan wondered out loud to John: what if she were to run away to Mexico? Pretty soon she was going to start to show, and then all hell would break loose with the authorities. Joan had a friend living in a tiny village south of Puerto Vallarta, and she could stay with him till she found her own place, just a hut. The money her father sent every month might even be enough to live on in Mexico. She would have the baby and raise her as a Mexican. Then an inspiration struck Jan: would John like to come with her? They could write a novel together, basing the characters on themselves and the style on that of Durrell's *Alexandria Quartet*, which John had encouraged her to read. What say? How about a big adventure with a pregnant teenager? Sure. Just the thing.

I'm sure Jan was astonished when John Lash accepted her offer. It was a dream come true. Who cared if the baby belonged to Michael? Jan and John would have other babies, and this one would be treated no differently than the ones that followed. Her mind worked overtime imagining the details of a simple life in Mexico. Back to the earth. America: love it or leave it. The time was ripe, and as Edgar observed to Lear, ripeness is all. Jan set Joan to writing to her contact, and her excitement infected her mother, who decided she would join them with David and the twins. John Aly had been pestering Joan for visitation privileges, which she had for some reason denied him, even after he came to New York in search of them. He hadn't seen his daughters in seven years. So Joan would have to make some arrangement with her estranged husband as well, before she could leave the country. Perhaps she would let their father take them for Thanksgiving, then she could lay her plans to follow Jan to Mexico.

And then Jan had another happy thought: Why not visit my father in Lowell? We can announce my pregnancy and fill him in on our plans at the same time. Perhaps he'll give us his blessing. John could hardly refuse, since the offer included an opportunity to meet the author who was already something of a cult figure, one many pundits held responsible for the growing turmoil among the nation's youth, added to his previous crimes in the Beat Generation. So when they left that fall of 1967, they headed not south, but north, to pay their respects to yet another absent father.

The story of Jan's second and last meeting with her father, repeated in most of the Kerouac biographies over the past twenty years, remains fairly stable. Jan and John arrive in Lowell on a cold November day, look up her name in the phone book, and get the number of Herve Kerouac, Jack's cousin. At Herve's house, his wife Doris observes the unmistakable resemblance of daughter to father, calls Jack, and sends the young couple on over to Sanders Avenue, where Jack and Stella are living in a new split-level home. Stella allows Jan to enter, but John stays outside until she can announce his presence to her father, who is sitting with his nose almost touching the TV screen, watching *The Beverly Hillbillies* and swigging intermittently from a bottle of scotch. Other relatives are milling around the house, and occasionally Jack shouts an unheeded order about the volume of the television, although he practically has his hand on the control knob. Gabrielle, who has suffered a stroke the year before, precipitated by the untimely death of her daughter, Caroline, lies virtually comatose on a daybed in the living room. At the sound of Jan's voice, the old lady stirs. "Is Carolyn here?" she inquires hopefully, referring to her dead daughter.

Jack finally turns, and his ice-blue eyes meet Jan's ice-blue eyes. Both father and daughter experience the mirroring effect, but the father turns away without a sign of recognition. He is hiding behind the alcohol, as he has done for many years with many other people. Jan asks if she can bring her boyfriend in out of the cold. John's hair has gotten a bit long, following the new fashion, but he is entering a conservative French-American home. Jack takes in his top-knot at a glance and says in a facetious tone, "Ah, it's Genghis Khan."

After half an hour Jan manages to break through the several barriers her father has erected around himself to announce her plans — her pregnancy must be obvious — to go to Mexico with John. They are going to write a novel together, she adds. "Good," Jack says, finally looking at her again. "You go to Mexico and write a book. You can use my name." It sounds as if he is giving her a gift, but then he inquires whether she has been receiving the $52 in child support he is required to send every month. It doesn't occur to her that he might be implying that she bears his name only as a result of legal compulsion, or that he might be wondering selfishly behind his alcoholic haze whether her pregnancy prefigures her marriage and thus the end of his financial responsibility, paltry though it is.

He turns his attention back to the adventures of the Clampett family in Hollywood. Jan's voice has caused Gabrielle to stir uneasily again, and Stella, understandably uncomfortable in Jan's presence, uses her mother-in-law as an excuse to expel the would-be daughter from the inner sanctum of the Kerouacs' conflicted home. Jan and John step back out into the brisk late autumn air, reorient themselves to the larger world into which they are about to adventure, and set off for Maine to bid farewell to John's family. Like Sal Paradise's first misstep in *On the Road*, the beginning of their long journey is taking them farther from their destination, but before they know it, their excitement has carried them back to New York, and they find themselves on a plane bound for Acapulco.

My description of Jan's experiences in Mexico depends partly on my interviews with her and partly on her own description of events in *Baby Driver*. I'm always suspicious of Jack's biographers when they summarize his own account of events without warning the reader. Like her father, Jan had an excellent memory of her own experiences, but also like Jack, she was capable of milking those events for their drama and humor, if not manipulating the details outright. The cover copy of the paperback edition of *Baby Driver* calls the book an "autobiographical novel," and this paradoxical subtitle points up one of the difficulties in writing about Jan or her father. Were they playing the age-old authorial trick of trying to convince the reader that nothing in the book is fabricated? Did they believe that words can convey the details of life without transforming them? How much did they alter or invent what they describe as personal experience?

To some extent, a historian or biographer can track down documents and witnesses that shed light on the veracity of a subjective account. This craving for comparisons has led to the production of nine biographies of Jack Kerouac in less than thirty years, quite a rate for an uncanonized author. But readers and fans have a sense that in understanding Jack's life they understand his works, just as in understanding his works they had developed a feeling for his life. Inevitably, the boundary between life and art becomes blurred, and perhaps that is just as well. In Jan's case, I suspect there is more reason to believe that her writing reflects the unvarnished truth, since she was neither as ambitious nor as well-read as her father. Even the structure of alternating two separate time lines in *Baby Driver*, she told me, was suggested by her first editor at St. Martin's Press. If she had read even her father's novels carefully, she might have hit on this simple strategy herself. At the time I was interviewing her, she was still working on her third book, *Parrot Fever*, and she seemed quite excited by the prospect of narrating one chapter from the point of view of a male character, as though the notion had never crossed her mind before. This authorial naïveté also makes me believe that much of what she says about herself is true. Remember, however, that her mother enjoyed reinventing herself and her past.

When Jan and John finally got settled on a dirt road in Yelapa, near Puerto Vallarta far down on Mexico's Pacific coast, they wrote to Joan and to Jack and to their friends to let everyone know they could be contacted by mail, which they would receive at the village store, the *tienda* of Juan Cruz. They missed Joan's friend, who had already moved farther south, and they needed Jack's child-support payments to cover their rent and put food on the table. Joan sent them a little money, but she had troubles of her own. At Thanksgiving her second husband had taken his twin daughters, now ten years old, and promptly shipped them off to live with his parents in Eugene, Oregon. If Joan wanted them back, she would have to fight a custody battle on the West Coast. Naturally, just getting there would take all her money, and regrettably, she would not be able to join Jan and John in Mexico to help Jan with her first baby. I marvel she ever believed that this was a feasible plan. In any event, the young couple settled into their hut — just the kind of existence Jack used to fantasize about during his frequent trips to Mexico during the 1950s — and Jan was quite pleased when the occasional tourist mistook her, with her long black hair and her peasant dress, for a native.

Jan and John began work on a novel together, using Durrell's plot and substituting themselves and their friends as characters. They called it, appropriately, *The Influence*. Jan became Justine for literary purposes, while John became Max and Michael Duarte was renamed Philip. Within ten weeks they had handwritten about 140,000 words. At the same time, they settled into a quiet routine, celebrating the *Navidad* and the *Año Nuevo* with the villagers. John began to build primitive furniture with just a machete for a saw and grass for twine. For a while — a very brief while — they lived out a hippie fantasy of simplicity. Jan, who had been coached in Spanish by her mother, quickly became fluent. The locals began to take them for granted. Money was scarce, but they made do, looking forward to the arrival of the baby in April. Then came the nightmare.

One night in early February, just a couple weeks before her sixteenth birthday, Jan woke in terror from a sound sleep. She felt as though an evil spirit was lurking just outside the door of their hut. Then the door rattled, and she screamed, waking John. He tried to calm her, reasoning that it was nothing more than the fruit bats that tried to raid their provisions every night. But during his travels in India, John had developed a healthy respect for occult powers, and he respected Jan's intuition about the danger of evil. Soon, however, his focus shifted to Jan herself, and he realized she was in pain. Her labor had begun; the baby was going to be two months premature. John ran out to fetch the midwife, determined to make the best of a bad situation, but by the time he returned with her to light a fire and prepare for the birth, Jan was in agony. When the baby came, it was not breathing. She, that is. Natasha. The next day, led by a procession of village youngsters, they laid the stillborn infant to rest in the local graveyard. Jan never forgot her Natasha, however, the closest she ever came to starting a family of her own.

By the time Jan had recovered sufficiently to travel, they had a letter from her mother informing them that Joan had moved to San Francisco, instead of going directly to Oregon. John determined that they should join her there, understanding that Joan could help Jan grieve and recover from the tragedy, he could easily find work, and they could join the growing number of young people seeking refuge in Haight-Ashbury. The couple set out for the border by bus, and by the time they reached Tijuana, Jan was so exhausted that John had to carry her to the American side. The next day they reached San Francisco, located Joan, and settled into her apartment on Laguna Street.

As Jan regained her strength, they began to explore the Haight, which was just a short bus ride up the hill from Joan's place. Jan began to take an interest in making jewelry, just as the skate punks of the 1990s string beads to sell to the tourists near the Panhandle. John landed an excellent job as a steelworker, and soon they had enough money to afford their own place. First, they occupied a small flat at 457 Oak Street, still in Joan's neighborhood, then, tiring of the street life on Haight, they chose an apartment across town on Utah Street, near Potrero Hill, the same neighborhood O. J. Simpson grew up in. Having started out as soul-mates, they felt their bond annealed by adventure, tragedy, and escape. Early in December they went to the opulent county courthouse and bought a marriage license, and on December 3, John's twenty-third birthday, they were married by a judge in one of the courtrooms. Joan had already moved north by this time, and a court clerk served as witness to the ceremony. Jan Kerouac was still only sixteen.

John Lash was always ahead of the trends in American culture, and in early 1969 he could easily see that San Francisco was becoming a parody of hippie life. Besides, the subculture was beginning to take a violently political cast in the wake of the Chicago Democratic Convention, and neither he nor his young wife, though clearly progressive, was ever very political. By spring they had determined to join Joan, who had settled in the Kittitas Valley in Washington with her son, David. Using their hippie connections, they began to work their way north from commune to commune through California wine country. Thirsty for more experience and not being in any particular hurry, they stayed till they tired of the company, or until their welcome wore out.

By October they had made it only as far as a small farm occupied by just one other couple near Little River. A photo from this period shows Jan in the garden, her black hair grown past her waist, in a sleeveless, flowered dress, her blue eyes as sharp as icepicks. I imagine her in this brown paradise of Northern California, all of seventeen, still partying hard, learning to live the rural life, enjoying both the security of marriage and the sexual freedom of the hippie lifestyle, when the second tragedy of her young life occurred. At the end of the third week of October, the woman they were living with came out of the house, where she was listening to the radio, to find Jan in the garden.

"I just heard on the news that your father died," the young woman said, tears streaming down her face. Jack Kerouac, the

Jan Kerouac as a hippie chick, circa 1970

King of the Beats, the Granddaddy of the Hippies, had quitted his mortal coil. Hardened by her experience in Mexico, Jan took the news unmoved. Only days later did it hit her that she would never see her father again, never come to know him as she had somehow always assumed she would. Now, she cried. Once again, in the face of tragedy, she and John fled to her mother for comfort.

SIX

A COUSIN IN A PARALLEL UNIVERSE

In early June 1948 Carolyn Blake, Jack Kerouac's only sister, went into labor for the first and last time in her life. The twins weren't due for six more weeks, so Carolyn's husband, Paul, drove her up to the Duke University hospital in Durham, about an hour's drive from their home in Kinston, North Carolina. On the morning of June 10, having discovered that Carolyn was suffering from toxemia, the doctors performed a cesarean section, hoping to save the lives of the babies and the mother.

Only one of the twins, both boys, survived. Peter was stillborn, but Paul Junior was rushed from the delivery room into the nursery, where he was placed in an incubator. Despite the odds against him (given the dangers of the new technology and the pitfalls that lie in wait for any preemie), he thrived. I caught up with him forty-seven years later, while he was living in a rented house just north of a little town just north of Sacramento, California. Over beers at his kitchen counter, Paul Blake Jr., looking tanned and fit despite the hard times he has suffered, recounted the story of his life.

Paul's father was a brilliant man. Raised by strict fundamentalist parents in the sandy flats of eastern North Carolina, he went off to Duke University, where he played football. When World War II finally involved the U.S., Paul Senior joined the army air corps and became a pilot. Amid the danger, confusion, and excitement of those years, he met and married Carolyn Kerouac, a young woman from an industrial town in northeastern Massachusetts, who had enlisted in the WACS after her first marriage to a French-Canadian boy from Lowell ended in an annulment, the Catholic's only alternative to divorce. Like her mother, Carolyn practiced a

Paul Blake in Rio Linda, CA, August 1995

perfervid form of French peasant Catholicism, which included special devotion to Ste. Thérèse, the Little Flower. Marriage to a Southern Protestant presented some obstacles, but Carolyn couldn't resist the handsome flyboy, and after her first failed attempt at marriage, she was eager to enjoy the romance, put the unrest of war behind her, and settle down to start a family.

Unlike most members of his mother's family, Paul Junior inherited fair hair. He resembled no one except his deceased uncle Gerard, Carolyn and Jack's saintly brother, who had died in 1926 of rheumatic fever at the tender age of nine. The likeness seemed almost miraculous to the Kerouac side of the family. Because of his reddish-blond hair, his grandmother Kerouac, Gabrielle, began right away to refer to little Paul as "her little golden boy." To her he seemed the reincarnation of the gentle son she had mourned twenty years before. The bond grew strong between grandmother and grandson, and according to Paul, remained unbroken until her death in 1973. The new baby also signified a shift in family roles, and Carolyn and Jack now began to call their mother "Mémêre," the French equivalent of "Granny." In 1995, when I interviewed him, Paul still evinced strong feelings for his Mémêre: "She never stopped loving me," he insisted.

Back home in Kinston in 1948, Mémêre joined her daughter's family to help with Carolyn's recuperation by taking care of her new — and as it turned out, only — grandson. Soon they were joined by Uncle Jack, who was just then completing his first published novel, *The Town and the City*, the fictional saga of the Martin family, with characters multiplied from the original five members of the Kerouac family. What's more, he had also begun his "research" on a new novel, one that eventually made him famous. He had recently returned from the first of many cross-country trips, and soon the flesh-and-blood model for the hero of that yet-to-be-written classic, Neal Cassady, would pay a surprise visit to the Blake family. (Years later at a fund-raiser for Jan Kerouac in San Francisco, Paul finally got a chance to meet Neal's son, John Allen, for whom he had always felt a strange affinity.) Little Paul's first Christmas was a real family affair, and in 1969, in his last letter to his nephew, Jack reminded Paul that the two of them were "of the same blood and also were good buddies and have an association that went back to when you were one year old."

Naturally, in the melding of families from such different backgrounds, tensions arose. "My dad was the tyrant of the family," Paul Junior said in 1995. "He was always in control. He forbade them to speak French. He got on Jack's ass." To a Southern WASP the boisterous Gallic temperament of the Kerouac clan seemed suspiciously frivolous, if not downright sinful. And to a military man, no less, Jack's chosen career seemed irresponsible, unproductive, and wasteful, especially in the vista of unlimited material prosperity presented by the post-war years. Paul Senior simply could not comprehend his brother-in-law's commitment to a field that offered such tenuous economic rewards. To a man trying to gain a foothold in the mushrooming economy — a man who turned even his hobby into a profitable sideline — Jack Kerouac looked at best like a good-for-nothing, at worst, a fool. In retrospect, Paul Junior described his father's attitude toward his wife's family this way: his mother-in-law was his nemesis, while his brother-in-law was a monkey on his back. With characteristic charity, however, Paul Junior concluded, "My dad was a military man and an asshole, but I loved him."

For all his rigidity, Paul Senior was a brilliant and practical man. He learned to fly in the army, where his mechanical aptitude quickly led him to learn the new field of electronics. By the time his son was born, Big Paul, as he now became known in the family, accurately perceived the fortune of the new medium and started his own business installing and repairing televisions in motels, bars, and other establishments. At home he raised bird dogs that were sought by hunters from as far away as Georgia and Kentucky. If he was chagrined by Jack's inability to hold a job or make money, Big Paul was simply astounded by Jack's ignorance of hunting skills. Little Paul recalled one occasion when his father took Jack out in the field. Of course, Jack didn't shoot a single bird — his tenderness for animals wouldn't have permitted him to kill a living creature even if he had been able to hit it — but he was impressed by the dogs his brother-in-law had raised and trained. "Those dogs are amazing," Jack kept repeating, as Big Paul just shook his head. In Jack's imagination, however, his country boy in-law sometimes became part of his scheme to buy a communal ranch out West, where his family would join the Cassadys in a pastoral romance.

Some readers have expressed surprise at a passage in the *Selected Letters* of Jack Kerouac in which Jack suggests that his sister act as his literary agent. Decades after the fact, Paul Blake shed some light on this situation. Nin had worked as a teacher before her marriage, and when her husband started their TV business, she kept the books. As royalties from Jack's modestly successful first novel trickled in, Jack began to express dissatisfaction with his agent, Sterling Lord. Nin seconded her brother's fears by suggesting that perhaps more careful accounting procedures were needed. To be fair, while she obviously knew little of the New York publishing world, it was not unreasonable of her to suspect that an agent might act unscrupulously. It had been known to happen, and it was in Nin's personal interest to make sure that her brother got every penny that was coming to him.

As far as her son is concerned, Carolyn Kerouac Blake was not only a woman of intelligence, but a very loving wife and mother as well. She made their home life fun, on the model of her parents' social life in Lowell during the Depression. "She was the most pleasant, fun-loving woman I've ever known," Paul said of his mother, describing his childhood environment as a "happy household." As upbeat as Carolyn tried to keep their daily doings, however, she couldn't help worrying about her kid brother. "She knew he was going to kill himself," Little Paul said in retrospect. In fact, just after his mother died of a coronary occlusion in 1964, Mémère had a dream about her. In the dream Nin laid her hand on her mother's arm and said, "I am in transition. I love you very much. Please take care of Ti Jean" (Jack's childhood nickname).

With his mother's sunny disposition and his father's practical outlook creating a pleasant, if imperfect, balance, Little Paul grew up sheltered and happy. He spent most of his time playing in the piney woods around their second home in Rocky Mount, near where his father's family lived. As an only child, his most frequent companions were his dogs, Min and Bill, and his uncle Jack. "He was my best friend," Paul still says today. One of his earliest memories is of Jack trying to feed him peanuts over Nin's protests. Later, as Little Paul grew out of infancy, Jack taught him how to play the baseball board game he had invented when he himself was a child. Jack always promised his nephew he could have the game someday.

On his visits to Rocky Mount, Jack roamed the woods with Little Paul and the dogs, affectedly smoking a corncob pipe. Occasionally, they would cut down a pine tree to make a "shade shelter." Jack reserved the more dramatic felling of the tree for himself, and Little Paul got stuck with the tedious job of trimming off the small branches. Often Jack would make him demonstrate his knot-tying skill by having him lace together the boughs of the downed tree. Eventually, after several long visits, Jack began to feel at home in North Carolina, relishing the contrast of the rich Southern dialect with that of his native New England. Often, when Little Paul turned in early for the night, Jack would walk to the country store in Little Easonburg to jaw with the storekeepers, George and John Langley. Eventually, Paul says, Jack knew as much about their business as the Langleys themselves, not to mention gathering quite a hoard of neighborhood gossip.

The family's idyllic country life began to change as the 1950s wore on. As Little Paul grew into boyhood, his father sensed that his hometown was not the best place to do business as the race for space commenced. With his buddy Wes Claus, Big Paul schemed about starting a company that would manufacture components for rocket and weapons telemetry and sell them to the government. About the same time, Jack's big novel, *On the Road*, which he had been reinventing regularly for almost a decade, finally hit the stands after languishing in his publisher's offices for several years. Suddenly, Paul's uncle was famous — or rather infamous — and all at once he began to have a substantial, if erratic, income. Then Paul's father spotted an opportunity.

A friend of Big Paul's, now a major in the Strategic Air Command, had been reassigned from North Carolina to Orlando, Florida. He wrote to his old buddy from the Civil Air Patrol that Florida was thriving. Because of the booming economy and the large military presence, Orlando seemed like the perfect spot for a budding military-industrial entrepreneur. Big Paul announced his decision to the family, and they were overjoyed. Mémère was getting old enough to feel the damp North Carolina winters, and Nin relished the idea of moving someplace with a bit more social life. For his part, Jack looked forward to buying his mother the first house she had ever owned. Only Little Paul left Rocky Mount with some regret. After all, it was the only life he had ever known, and his had been a storybook boyhood. As a condition of moving, he made his father promise to load the quarter-midget race car he had built for him into their station wagon so the movers wouldn't damage it. Big Paul magnanimously consented, perhaps because only the backseat passengers would be inconvenienced. On a bright, sunny day in 1958, the Kerouac/Blake clan climbed in the Ford and began the long drive to Orlando.

Life in the Sunshine State took a shape none of the family could have predicted at that moment, least of all ten-year-old Paul. First, since Jack was flush for the first time in his life, and Big Paul needed money to start his new venture — despite the capital he brought from the sale of the TV business in Rocky Mount — he borrowed $5,500 from his lazy brother-in-law. That was a large sum in those low-inflation days, and Big Paul never paid it all back. For the penny-pinching Kerouac the money became a bone of contention in the family during the next few years. In his last letter to Little Paul, written the day before he died, Jack bequeathed his nephew what his father owed him: "Don't let Big Paul, your Pop think that he can get anything out of this as he owes me $5,500, but it's for you, just for the blood of it." But if Jack forgave — though he never forgot — this sentence embarrassed Little Paul (who was fully grown when he first read it), and he subsequently blotted out the line to protect his father's reputation.

Soon the family had settled in a new subdivision in Orlando, but not all in the same house. Big Paul wanted his privacy, and his prospects certainly indicated that he would soon be able to afford it. He settled his wife and son in their new home, and Jack and Mémère moved in next door. At the very moment his words began to inspire countless Americans to leave the stodgy security of suburbia, the author whose characters seemed to remain in constant motion came to rest in one of America's newly built tract houses. As if to underscore this irony, Jack's old traveling buddy, Neal Cassady, got busted in California for giving a few joints to some undercover cops who gave him a ride to work. Soon, greasers wearing Dharma Bums jackets began to arrive unannounced on the doorstep of Jack's new home, but what they found was not the model of Sal Paradise or Ray Smith, but an increasingly bitter man slipping into middle age.

For a while Little Paul remained oblivious to these changes. His dad had promised to let him drive his quarter-midget on the beach at Daytona, site of the famous speedway, and he kept his word. His son still recalls the thrill of that ride. But Big Paul went his son one better: he bought an old flathead Ford engine, scrounged some airplane tires, and cobbled together a primitive dune buggy, so he could take his son on even more exciting rides along the beach. Eventually, Big Paul also bought a little British sports car, still quite exotic in the late 1950s, which because of the configuration of its headlights was called a "bug-eyed" Sprite. There were lots of new, curvy roads with no houses on them in their subdivision, and in just a few years Little Paul began sneaking the car out when his father was away, picking up Uncle Jack, and racing around late at night. Together they discovered a long, vacant straightaway, and Jack bought a stopwatch so he could clock his nephew's speed in the quarter-mile.

Soon it became easier for Little Paul to get out alone, because after his father's plans to start his own company failed to materialize, he took a job with the Pentagon installing weapons systems at military bases all over the country. Though this required Big Paul to go where the work was, the money was excellent and he was able to employ many of his varied mechanical skills, so gradually, almost imperceptibly, he began to lose touch with his wife and son.

Big Paul didn't worry too much about being away. After all, his wife's mother lived right next door, and Mémère was both practical and protective. Besides, Uncle Jack was around more often than not these days, and after an abortive attempt to move his mother to California, he seemed to accept the notion that she would live out her days in the Florida warmth. He still went off to carouse with his old friends, but the scene in New York City or San Francisco did not excite him as it had in the old days. Usually Jack wound up on a binge, after which he was glad to get home to rest and write, aided and diverted by the attentions of his family. Little Paul became the son Jack never had but always wanted. Later Paul explained his uncle's failures in marriage in terms of Jack's parents: "The life Leo and Mémêre had was so endearing that he could never find it. He had an idea of how family life should be." And he himself could never live up to it.

Jack Kerouac may have failed to father his own son, but he was not without offspring, Little Paul discovered. One day in 1961, when Paul was twelve, Jack returned from a mysterious trip to New York. The boy hurried next door to see if his uncle had brought him anything from the city, and they were sitting in the living room shooting the breeze when Jack suddenly pulled out his wallet. Apropos of nothing, he extracted a snapshot of a dark-haired little girl riding a tricycle. Her small face looked strikingly like Jack's. "I have a daughter," was all he said.

"So that's my cousin?" Little Paul asked excitedly, expecting to hear more about his newfound relative, who was then almost nine years old. Jack put his finger to his lips, warning the boy to keep the news to himself. But Mémêre had overheard them.

Jan Kerouac, June 1956

Suspicious, she burst into the living room, just as Jack was hastily replacing the photo (which his ex-wife Joan Haverty had given him). Immediately, she understood what had passed between uncle and nephew, and she flew into a rage. She shouted at her son in French, "Your mouth is full of shit! Why do you tell him such lies?"

Jack's tone changed abruptly, and he began to respond in kind: "If my mouth is full of shit, and I came out of you, then you must be full of shit, too." As their words grew coarser and more heated, Paul's comprehension diminished rapidly, to his relief. Pretty soon, all the language escaped him, but Mémêre's motive remained clear the rest of his life: she refused to admit that Jack had fathered a child and then abandoned it, even though at least on that day, the father himself seemed not only to admit paternity, but to take a strange, secret pride in it.

The reason for Jack's trip to New York that January 1961, as we know, was that he had been summoned by Joan Haverty to submit to a blood test to determine whether or not he was the father of her first child, Janet Michele. The tests showed that he probably was, or at least that his blood type showed that he could be the father. (Other candidates were never tested, so far as I know.) Many years later, when the first cousins finally got in touch in early 1995, Jan sent Paul some photographs from her childhood. As they were discussing them on the phone, Jan asked if Paul had noticed one of her, age four, riding a tricycle. "Yes," he replied, adding, to her surprise, "but I've seen that one before."

Paul Blake Jr. said years later that he wasn't surprised that Jack had a child. In fact, he says he'd be surprised if Jan were his only child. When I asked him why he thought Jack revealed his secret to him when he did, Paul told me he thought it had something to do with the birds and the bees. Jack sensed that his nephew was growing into manhood, and telling him he had a daughter was his way of explaining the facts of life. If the lesson was a bit indirect, at least Jack's timing was right. Before long, Paul was going to need all the help he could get, not just to understand what was happening to his own body, but to make sense of the growing strain on his parents' marriage.

As the arms race escalated in the wake of the Cuban missile crisis, Big Paul found his services more and more in demand at the Pentagon. He traveled more frequently and stayed away for longer periods of time. For a while husband and wife traveled together, establishing temporary homes in apartments in Chicago and Seattle, but the strain of moving drove Nin back to Florida to be with her son and her mother. Eventually, perhaps inevitably, Big Paul found female companionship on the road. Carolyn, always a devout Catholic and made more sensitive by her first failed marriage, was devastated by her husband's affair, and when he finally asked her for a divorce, she was crushed. In her mind, divorce was not an option. What would she do? What would become of her son? Unable to remarry, this true family woman would be forced to live without a companion for the rest of her life. The stress affected her health, and she stopped eating properly. Within a few short years she developed high blood pressure, and in September 1964, she suffered the heart attack that took her life. She was only forty-five years old.

Everyone in the family was stunned by Carolyn's premature death, including her ex-husband. According to his son, Paul Blake Sr. never recovered from his belief that he had caused his first wife's death. Despite his new marriage to Joyce, a woman he had met in southern California, and his successful career, Big Paul began to drink heavily, and in less than ten years, he, too, would die. The death of the second of her three children brought equally severe consequences for Mémère as well. Always a sturdy woman, she had, nevertheless, reacted physically to Gerard's death in 1926: all her teeth had fallen out. Now, almost forty years later, this new tragedy would precipitate a stroke in only two years.

The effect on Jack, if less noticeable and less immediate, was no less profound. "When my mom died," Paul Blake Jr. said in 1995, "he gave up. He didn't want to live." Jack's grief was compounded both by his mother's illness and by the hostile, dismissive attitude of critics toward his writing. Not only was he suddenly forced to care for the woman who had always cared for him, but he was also compelled to face the possibility that his revolutionary writings of the 1950s had been merely a flash in the pan, doomed to oblivion by reactionary, uncomprehending hacks. If he had always been a heavy drinker, Jack now began in earnest the agonizing process of killing himself with booze.

During and after the breakup of Nin and Paul's marriage, Jack tried hard to act as surrogate father to Little Paul. He continued to coach his nephew in football and track, at which Jack had once excelled. Sometimes Jack walked down to Paul's high school near the end of the final period. When Paul emerged from the main doors he'd spot his uncle reclining on the lawn in front of the building, peacefully smoking a cigarette at the foot of a "Keep Off the Grass" sign.

But Jack's own worries, both personal and professional, outstripped his ability to function as a parent, either for his nephew or his daughter, who by this time had already dropped out of high school and gotten heavily involved in the drug scene on the Lower East Side. Possibly in imitation of his father's many moves during Jack's childhood, possibly to please his mother's whims, or possibly to simply distract himself from his troubles, Kerouac began to move erratically, searching for the perfect place to find peace to write and to protect his ailing mother.

Other events also conspired to separate uncle and nephew. After his mother died, Little Paul begged his father to let him stay with Jack and Mémêre, so he could finish his last two years of high school in Orlando. Maybe now that he was old enough to drive, he could chauffeur his uncle on another of his notorious cross-country adventures. Jack seemed willing enough, but Big Paul asserted his paternal authority with typical military discipline. His son was still a minor, and as such he had little choice but to obey the man whom he now regarded as the cause of his mother's death, if not the disintegration of his entire family. So in 1965, with his North Carolina boyhood rapidly receding under the pressure of adult decisions, Paul Blake Jr. left his beloved grandmother and uncle, his high school pals, and his second home to move three thousand miles to live with his estranged father and "the other woman" on the West Coast. Just to make sure his son didn't change his mind at the last minute, Big Paul threatened to have the police escort him to the airport.

When he moved to San Pedro, California, to join his father and stepmother, Little Paul (no longer little by this time) tried hard to keep doing the things he had always liked to do. He began his junior year at South Torrance High School. He went out for football and made the varsity team, winning the starting wing-back position. Much like his uncle at Lowell High School thirty years before, he also ran track. Before he could get settled, however, his father announced yet another change: they were moving to Anchorage, Alaska. Paul wrote to Mémère and Jack, who had just sold their house in Florida and moved back North to Massachusetts, where they bought a house in Hyannis. Both his grandma and his uncle missed their Ti Paul as much as he missed them, and they invited him to spend part of his summer with them on Cape Cod. Partly to please his son and partly to ease the difficulty of moving, Big Paul gave his permission, and soon after school let out for the summer, his son flew to Boston, making the last leg to Hyannis by bus.

Back on the East Coast Paul reveled in his uncle's company and basked in his grandmother's love. Even though Jack was obviously suffering as his relation with his mother changed him into the caregiver — drinking more heavily than ever and quarreling more viciously with Mémère, who had begun to show clear signs of old age — Paul managed to revive some of the old feeling of comradeship. His visit turned into a combination of vacation and reunion of the diminished Kerouac clan.

One day, Paul recalls, a stranger came to visit. An attractive, dark-haired woman pulled into the drive shortly after noon in a shiny Volkswagen Beetle with a big Irish setter crammed into the tiny backseat. Jack was obviously expecting her, and Mémère and her grandson stood together in the kitchen as Jack opened the door for Ann Charters, who had come to work with him on a bibliography of his published writing. With his lingering dreams of conventional literary fame, Jack was honored to be visited by a scholar with a Ph.D. from Columbia. Paul had brought his dad's Super-8 movie camera along on his trip, and when Ann and Jack emerged from Jack's study, he filmed Mémère giving Jack a haircut. In the process he caught the future biographer and founder of Kerouac studies on his home movie as well.

When Ann went out to retrieve her dog, who had been left in the yard to avoid disturbing the Kerouac cats, she inquired of Mémère whether the dog had caused any problems. The old lady told her it had dug up some plants in the garden. Clearly concerned that the dog might have worn out her welcome, Ann offered to replace the plants the next day, if Mémère would tell her what kind they were. Looking straight into her eyes the matriarch replied, without a trace of irony, "Wandering Jew."

After Ann left and Mémère cleared away the dinner dishes, Little Paul offered his uncle a glass of iced tea. Jack declined, saying, "I like to drink hot things when it's hot and cold things when it's cold."

"That doesn't make sense," the nephew shot back.

"Neither does that woman who was just here," Jack retorted. As Paul marveled at the way his uncle had set him up, Jack added with a wink, "Besides, she's a piss-poor lay." The eighteen-year-old took his word for it, just as he had taken Jack's word that he had fathered a daughter.

In the morning Ann Charters, ignorant of houseplants, went to a nursery and asked hesitantly for wandering Jew. She was in luck; the greenhouse had plenty. She bought a whole flat and placed it in the passenger seat of her V-dub, where the dog couldn't get at it. When she arrived at the Kerouac home, she knocked on the door a second time and, to her inward delight, Jack's mother answered the door. "Here's your wandering Jew," Ann announced, mustering her most innocent smile and straining not to burst out laughing.

A few days later Little Paul reluctantly left Jack and Mémère for his new home in Anchorage. His father had already enrolled him at East Anchorage High School, where he would complete his senior year. When he got settled back at his dad's new home, the first thing the young man did was talk to the high school football coach. To his dismay, however, Paul found that sports programs in the forty-ninth state lagged far behind those in Southern California, and perhaps for reasons he did not fully comprehend at the time, he decided not to try out for the team. Instead he spent his senior year trying unsuccessfully to crack the established cliques in his new school.

Before he knew it, Paul Blake Jr. was a high school graduate and prime candidate for the draft into the escalating Vietnam War. His father, understandably, encouraged him to join the air force, but the son, also understandably, wanted to enjoy his first taste of adult freedom. His Uncle Jack, much to his nephew's surprise, had remarried — to a sister of one of his high school buddies. Jack had known Stella Sampas all his life. The big sister of his highly literate buddy Sammy, who had died in North Africa during World War II, Stella had remained single, some said saving herself for Jack. Little Paul was anxious to meet his new aunt, renew his ties to Jack and Mémère, and visit some of his old high school friends in Florida. He had plenty of reasons to leave Alaska and make the five-thousand-mile trip from one corner of North America to the other, but his father pressed him for a more practical decision, and it took Paul Junior more than a year to act on his urge to travel, by which time his uncle, aunt, and grandmother had relocated to Florida.

Unbeknownst to Paul, Jack had received a surprise visitor in November 1967. Jan Kerouac, fifteen and pregnant, had made a special trip to Lowell to tell her father she was heading for Mexico. She brought along her twenty-one-year-old boyfriend, who became her first husband just over a year later. Preoccupied as she was with her own predicament, Jan was still overwhelmed by being in the presence of so many members of her father's side of the family. She had never experienced the warm, noisy, French-American sociability.

Jan found Jack in much the same state Paul later observed in Florida: swigging from a bottle of whiskey, watching TV amid the din, and shouting orders to anyone who'd listen. Mémère, whose mind seemed to Jan to be slipping, heard Jan's voice from the bedroom where she was resting. Through the chaos of conversation and blaring TV, what registered in the matriarch's dimming consciousness was the sound of her daughter's voice, for which she had apparently mistaken the voice of the granddaughter she had always refused to acknowledge. "Carolyn," Mémère murmured. Stella, sensing trouble, rushed the young couple out the door, leaving Mémère wondering if perhaps she'd been revisited by Carolyn's ghost.

In September 1968, at Mémêre's request, Jack moved his wife and mother south to St. Petersburg. By this time the Vietnam War had heated to the boiling point, and soon the draft lotteries would give young men a quantifiable means of gauging the proximity of the conflict to their own lives. As Paul cast about for some meaningful work to do, he discussed with his dad the possibility of joining the armed services. Paul Senior was, of course, all in favor of his son's going off to fight for his country. Little Paul still regularly called his grandmother and uncle, and Jack counseled him to avoid the draft and combat duty by joining the National Guard. Sometimes, however, Aunt Stella refused to put Jack or Mémêre on the phone. Jack was drunk, she told Little Paul, and Mémêre was resting. Occasionally, Paul got disturbing letters from Jack, in which his uncle made wild accusations that Stella was poisoning him.

To say that Paul was nervous and exhilarated by the prospect of returning to Florida is an understatement. He was truly on his own for the first time in his life. He was headed back to his old stomping grounds for the first time in three years. And he was going to meet his new Aunt Stella.

What he found in St. Pete dismayed him. Unlike during the relatively happy times in Orlando, Uncle Jack now sat in a rocking chair placed in the middle of the living room with a pitcher of water on one side of him and a big bottle of Johnnie Walker Red Label on the other, spitting out orders to his new wife. Likewise, Mémêre, whose health had continued to decline, made her own demands on Stella. More often than not, she demanded that her daughter-in-law bring her a cigarette and a glass of brandy, which she kept stashed side by side in a dresser drawer in her bedroom. Privately, she confided to her nephew about Stella, "She doesn't care for me." To make matters worse, she habitually referred to Stella as "Jackie's trash," which Paul took to mean that Mémêre thought Jack and Stella had slept with each other years ago back in Lowell. Altogether, it was not a pretty picture, and Paul felt more of his old family life slipping away before his very eyes.

Jack still managed to write a bit, and he had become even more interested in his own amateurish painting. Paul watched fascinated as Jack worked on a full-length portrait of the current pope, the progressive John XXIII. When he did go out of the house, he went out to drink with new friends in the bars in Tampa. Sometimes he came home considerably the worse for wear. His old friends had abandoned him to booze, and Jack reviled them for it. One day he showed Paul a mock-up for the cover of his new novel, *Vanity of Duluoz*, a collage in which Allen Ginsberg's head appeared to be growing out of Jack's armpit. "That's where that bastard belongs," Jack growled.

But Paul was now too full of the independent spirit to be troubled by the situation, and he was anxious to get on with his life. After a sad parting from his grandmother and from Jack, whom he never saw again, the young adventurer set out on his own road trip, visiting friends in Southern California before returning to his father's home in Alaska.

It took Paul almost another year before he decided to join the air force. Perhaps he would follow in his father's footsteps, but at the very least, the service would provide him with more job training, which would come in handy when he re-entered the labor market. When his orders finally came in the fall of 1969, Paul found himself bound for basic training in San Antonio, Texas.

Near the end of October he got another troubling letter from his Uncle Jack, forwarded from Anchorage. This one was half transcription of a warm greeting from his grandmother (she dictated to her son in French so Stella wouldn't understand), who was apparently too feeble to write. Thinking Paul was still up north, she asked him to send her a photo of himself in an Eskimo suit, inquired about his love life, and invited him to visit them again in Florida, so she could "renew the instincts she had felt with his mother." The disturbing part of the letter was that Jack told his nephew that he intended to divorce his wife and that he had made a new will leaving everything to Little Paul. Jack even mentioned the ten-year-old debt owed him by Big Paul. To a young man bound for service in an extremely hot war, it wasn't the most calming kind of family communication.

A few weeks later Paul learned that his uncle was dead. Jack had bled to death in a St. Petersburg hospital only a day after writing to Paul. Jan, who had returned to the United States after a harrowing six months in Mexico, heard the news of her father's death on the radio. It never occurred to her the previous fall that she might never see her father again. Little Paul, who had lived his early adolescence with Jack as a substitute father, took the news hard — harder than his cousin perhaps, since Jan had barely known Jack. But despite his grief, he forced himself to pay attention to his training, and before he knew it, he was fueling fighter planes in South Vietnam.

SEVEN

THE PROSTITUTE AS PIRATE

Just at the close of her chaotic teenage years in 1971, Jan Kerouac moved to Santa Fe, New Mexico, to start her adult life. Her first husband, John Lash, had just had an affair while they were living in Ellensburg, Washington. In the next chapter I expand on Jan's account in her 1981 novel, *Baby Driver* (republished in a new edition in the summer of 1998), in which she described the events that led to her first move to the Southwest, where she returned once again after suffering total kidney failure in Puerto Rico in 1991. But before continuing the course of Jan's life, I want to pause to include some of her own words.

On Friday, March 12, 1995, the seventy-third anniversary of her father's birth, Jan and I and photographer Sam Lines drove up to Santa Fe to visit some of Jan's old haunts, hoping it would spark her memory of past events, and to do a photo shoot. That night, back in Albuquerque, I concluded a weeklong series of interviews with her in preparation for a book on her life. This discussion — virtually the last lengthy talk I ever had with Jan — concerned her brief life as a prostitute in 1972 and 1973, after John Lash had rejoined her in the Southwest. Without any prompting on my part, Jan connected her sexual activities with the absence of her father and the much later onset of her kidney failure.

As March 12 turned into the thirteenth, I had no sense that anything had changed. Jan spoke openly and intelligently about this period of her life. Later, transcribing this interview, I was impressed by how much courage and conviction Jan showed as a young woman, abandoning a lucrative career before it damaged her severely. The next morning, however, after a few hours' sleep, I realized the interview had altered our relationship completely. From a position of growing trust and confidence, I was now

Jan Kerouac in Albuquerque, NM, March 1995

quickly reduced to the role of voyeur and traitor. Then in the midst of litigation against the heirs of her father's estate, from which she had been totally excluded, Jan feared that her forth-right admission of illicit behavior, even though it was by this time over twenty years in the past, would damage her chances of winning the lawsuit. As far as I know, it never became an issue in her deposition in January 1996, but I was subsequently contacted by a lawyer for the Sampas estate, who informed me very frankly that my tapes might be subpoenaed. I asked the lawyer to try to avoid using the information I had gathered for two reasons. First, I had obtained it in good faith, and I felt it would be wrong for Jan's own honesty with me to be used against her. Second, selfishly, I did not want the transcripts entered into the public record where anyone could obtain access to material that I had worked — and in some sense suffered — to gather. At last the Sampas lawyer, Lettie Marques, graciously offered to work around my tapes, but she warned me that if her client ordered her to subpoena my information, she would have no choice. I told her I understood perfectly.

The parts I've read of Jan's deposition in the lawsuit are brutal, not because of any nastiness on the part of Marques, but simply because they exposed Jan's fragility in what turned out to be the last few months of her life. More than anything else, the deposition revealed the seriousness of her illness. To attribute Jan's frequent confusions and evasions to anything but medication and fatigue would be a mistake, for as I saw for myself in March 1995, whatever the original cause of her kidney failure, the disease had left her the mere shell of her former self. As I read over her words to me on that fateful night for the umpteenth time, I am struck once again by what a strong, intelligent self it was that had been destroyed by deprivation, denial, carelessness, and just plain wild living. As she had followed her father in so many other ways, Jan also emulated Jack Kerouac in the end, dying an ugly, senseless, probably preventable yet absolutely inescapable death.

What follows is my transcription of the words we spoke that night. Ellipsis dots indicate a hesitation on the speaker's part. Ellipsis dots in brackets indicate that I have deleted irrelevant comments.

JAN: Well, I could sort of try to explain what it's like — what it was like to you, if you want.

JIM: Well . . .

JAN: That would be an interesting interview.

JIM: Yeah.

JAN: I know what it was like.

JIM: Well, what was it like? [. . .] You did it to begin with to make money, for John [Lash], didn't you?

JAN: Not for John, no.

JIM: I thought he needed three hundred dollars.

JAN: Oh. I forgot about that.

JIM: You describe it in *Baby Driver*.

JAN: Oh, that's right. OK. But I didn't tell him.

JIM: No, but . . .

JAN: But it was like a secret. Oh, now that's an interesting dynamic. [. . .] I really loved him and cared about him, as I still do, and always did, and he was pissed at me for a number of things. Um . . .

JIM: But mainly what?

JAN: That's one of the things I've never quite figured out is what happened with our relationship.

JIM: It seemed like everything was going pretty well in Washington.

JAN: I know.

JIM: Until he started sleeping with that woman you call Jenny [in the novel].

JAN: Yeah. Um.

JIM: Then he laid some kind of hippie rap on you at the time, didn't he? Like "We have to share ourselves"?

JAN: Yeah, something like that. But he was probably making it up as he went along.

JIM: You didn't buy it, did you? It didn't sound like it.

JAN: Uh, then again, I also doubted my own reasons for not buying it, because I thought maybe it was just because I was jealous. And we hadn't really experimented with any of this stuff before, you know, these feelings of possessiveness.

JIM: So from the time that you and John left New York to go to Mexico, you were faithful to each other.

JAN: Yeah. Until her. And that was like about two years. Or more.

JIM: A long time, during which time you bore a stillborn child.

JAN: Which was somebody else's.

JIM: Yeah, which was somebody else's. That seems like a really noble thing for him to do: to go with you and protect you.

JAN: Yeah. He didn't care. He just really liked me for me, and it didn't matter that I was pregnant with the devil. [Laughs] Well, anyway . . .

JIM: With some Mayan demon.

JAN: Well, actually by Michael Duarte, who lived next door [in New York City], the little hash-dealer guy. Anyway . . .

JIM: Anyway, we got kind of off the track. I'm sure that it crosses a lot of people's minds: Hey, I could go out and sell myself and make a lot of money.

JAN: Sure, but I think most women have been brought up with all these rigid principles and values that keep them from actually doing it, because they think, "Oh, that would be bad. I wouldn't do that, because then everyone would see me as being bad." And I really . . . I guess I didn't care. Well, I had a different kind of warped values, in which I thought it would be sort of heroic or interesting or entertaining, since I never had those foundations of anyone teaching me about morals. My mother basically just was my great friend and confidant, who . . . who, uh, well a few times she got really angry about Paul [one of Jan's first lovers] and tried to keep me from . . . But there was no way she could keep me from taking drugs, because she really couldn't control my actions. Anyway, I knew that, and so I was sort of saying, "Hah hah hah hah hah, I can do anything I want." Which was cruel of me, but most adolescents go through that. And then, then I found who I thought was my ultimate . . . you know . . .

JIM: True love.

JAN: Uh, companion, yeah. Besides her. In fact, at that point John and my mother and David [her brother] were my three most important people in my life right then. Now, still John and David. My mother's gone, and there's been some more people added to kind of fill in the gap she left, I guess, except . . . Well, anyway. So I'd like to just sort of start describing that, when I left the house, the little place I was living in Santa Fe, and venture out at night and go to the Forge. That was the first place I really did it.

JIM: And that's the place that we saw today that's catty-corner from the state capitol.

JAN: That's the thing. Legislators. All the guys who were in the legislature would . . . In fact, there's a whole period of time called "legislature." That's right. I don't know exactly what month it is now, but all the guys, all the politicians, would come and have drinks over there. And you know how they are. They're always looking for some kind of bimbos to fool around with. Traditionally, I guess. And so there I was. That's the thing. I even wrote this in *Baby Driver*, and I just remembered it. There was some guy that I met — I don't even know who it is now, who it was — who said to me, "Hey, I tell you what. You need money?" Oh, right, 'cause I was trying to get money, and I was asking everybody.

JIM: Now say that again. You met somebody . . .

JAN: I met some guy, and I can't remember who, but he was like a drinking buddy or a guy who was in the pool halls, and I said, "Hey, you know, I've got to make three hundred dollars fast, like this week." And he said to me, "Oh. Yeah. If you want to make three hundred dollars, I'll tell you what to do." He was very matter-of-fact and very sort of teachy about it. He said, "Just go down to the Forge. Get yourself all dolled up and go down to the Forge tonight. Sit at the bar and just make a proposition." Oh, he said, "See how many propositions you can make." And I said, "Propositions?" I was kind of dumb about it. I said, "Propositions? What do you mean?" And he explained what he meant. "You know. Pick up some guys and go with them to their rooms and, uh, see how much money I could make." And so I thought, "OK. I'll try that." Duh. Like whatchamacallit. What's that guy's name? "Shazam, shazam." The guy, uh, Gomer Pyle. [Imitating Gomer's voice] All right, I'll try it. I'll try anything once. [. . .] But you see, Gomer Pyle wouldn't have done that. He was too moral. [. . .]

[Sam Lines, the photographer, enters the room.]

JAN: Hi, we're talking about prostitution. [. . .]

JIM: In fact, we were talking about prostitution, and she was just going to tell me . . . she was just saying about her first experience going down to a place called the Forge.

JAN: Which I sort of mentioned today while we were walking.

SAM: You mentioned a guy looking out of the window.

JAN: Oh, him. No, that was before then.

JIM: That was before then?

JAN: Yeah, that was just a little affair that I had with him. That's the thing. Now this is another funny thing I just remembered. See, I was just having this affair with him. And I like him and he was cool and interesting and all that, and, uh, but somebody else told me, say, "Hey, see how much money you can get outta him." And I thought, "Oh." 'Cause I was really naive and I hadn't even thought of that at all. I just liked him.

JIM: Did he give you money?

JAN: No, but I suppose if I had asked him, he would've, because he would've been afraid I'd say something, get him in trouble, I guess. But my mind wasn't working that way. I just liked him, because he was handsome and all, and he said that he was French-Indian, and we were both French-Indian descent, you know. And we had fun together. And also it was kind of secretive and sort of exciting because I . . .

JIM: He was married, I presume.

JAN: Oh yeah. With kids. Probably. I didn't even really know.

JIM: [. . .]

JAN: And he is, he's still . . . I recently heard during this big election last year, I did hear his name a few times, so I guess he's still around here. He was the attorney general.

JIM: Wow!

JAN: That was the thing. Now I remember. Attorney general of New Mexico, and he was running for the senate, but I don't know if he ever got in or not. Maybe he did, in which case now he's a senator.

JIM: Good Lord!

JAN: I don't know what he is. [Laughs.]

JIM: Well, anyway, so you were starting to think about the sex-money equation.

JAN: Yeah. People were actually putting it in my mind. Maybe it was already there, but they just sort of jogged it a little bit. But then when I found out that John was destitute, suddenly I had this real mission, this reason for wanting to make money real fast, 'cause I wanted to give it to him. And I wanted to say, "Here, John. Like a gift, you know. 'Cause I don't want you to fall through the cracks or turn into a pauper or something." 'Cause I really, truly cared about him, but I also liked the idea of being this sort of lady of the night, kind of secretively, and the idea that I wouldn't tell him where I got it. But somehow or other I wound up admitting where I got it, and that angered him, I'm sure. It made him feel really bad because, of course, he didn't want to take money from that. From me, especially.

JIM: Sort of like being a pimp.

JAN: Yeah, it probably made him feel really low. And I started to realize that as things were happening. Somehow or other I just blocked it out, and I decided, well, I like doing this, 'cause this is the easiest way I've ever made money.

JIM: Do you remember the first night that you went down to the Forge and took the guy's advice and sat around and waited?

JAN: Visually, I remember what it looked like and felt like in there. It was very dark, a very dark lounge. Very large. I went up and sat at the bar. And it was just like magic. It was just like he said. Of course, I was really pretty then, too. I was only twenty, and I had long hair, and I was all made-up, and I was wearing this long, slinky red dress. And I just sat there, and in about two seconds, this businessman-looking guy came right over and sat right next to me. And you know, well, nowadays, I would think it's the oldest line in the book, 'cause it's happened to me many times over now. Now it's even stupid. I mean, the way I look at it is, "Oh, get out of here." You know, I'm not even interested. Well, I'm celibate now. But then it was like, "Oh, this is fun," you know, and flattering. Here's a guy, he's a sort of fatherly look- ing guy, who was obviously one of those politicians, and sure enough, just like this friend of mine said, he came right over. And he knew what he wanted, and he figured I was just playing the same game. We didn't really have to explain much. And then the alcohol helps. You sit there and flirt, and pretty soon he says, "Well, uh, let's go . . ." I don't know if he said let's go to my room, but he said let's go somewhere — but we knew he meant his room, so we went to his room. This fellow, this friend of mine, had even gone so far as to explain how to deal with the money part of it, so that it doesn't have to be construed as illegal. All you do is — Let's see, what did he say? Well, after you consummate the act, or whatever, you . . . See, if I told him to leave money on the dresser . . . Oh, I'd say something about "Yeah, just leave it over on the dresser.'' Then what happens is I get up at some point and pick it up, so it's not really exchanging hands. That's the whole thing. That supposedly . . .

JIM: So, like he just forgot the money?

JAN: Yeah. He knew that anyway. The guy just put it on the dresser, and I just took it,

JIM: So you weren't nervous?

JAN: A hundred dollars.

JIM: A hundred bucks the first time you turned a trick?

JAN: Yeah.

JIM: Nineteen seventy-two?

JAN: Yeah, so then . . . there was one time I got as much as, let's see . . . Oh, there was one time when I actually came down to Albuquerque here, I just remembered. There was this oil-millionaire guy, old and decrepit, very, very old. Couldn't do anything. Just a poor old guy, you know, with a lot of money. And somehow, it was getting really sort of slick at this point, like. I don't know who exactly was orchestrating things, but all I know is that it was arranged. It was like a real kinda high-class call-girl thing, where I walked into the Hilton, and let's see, what happened? Oh, right. I went and I spent the night, the whole night, with this old, weaselly guy.

JIM: Remember what his name was?

JAN: No, I don't think I ever knew. I came down. I was walking through the lobby, and I just sort of knew everything was happening, was gonna happen. I wasn't really worried. And sure enough, this guy, the businessman sort of guy from the Hilton, who was like part of the Hilton staff, came up to me and just very casually handed me this envelope. And I said thank you and I didn't even look in it. And later on I walked away and I opened it up and it was in a money thing. It was five hundred dollars. And so I thought, "Wow! Well, that was easy.'' I mean, I didn't have to do anything, because the guy was just too old.

JIM: So he just wanted someone to sleep with?

JAN: Yeah. And companionship. And I thought, "Well, that's great!'' You know, so I kept getting a bigger, inflated ego about this, thinking, "Hey, this is big time. I'm making money and not really doing much for it and having fun.''

JIM: I'm still curious about that first night, though. Would that have been, say, right around like late winter or early spring of 1972[–1973]?

JAN: I think it was probably spring.

JIM: Like right after your birthday? 'Cause you went to Phoenix in the summer of that year.

JAN: That's right, and this is all sort of leading up to going to Phoenix. [. . .] Anyway, you can sort of see, though it might be hard to imagine, since I didn't have any morals or values to begin with there was nothing in me that was saying, "This is wrong," 'cause no one had ever said that to me.

JIM: I can understand. It seems kind of heroic.

JAN: But I sort of knew also, I sort of knew in my bones that it was wrong. Not only just wrong, but also . . . [. . .] I think I had a suspicion that it was bad for me physically and also emotionally, and yet because I was drinking, that provided the shield for that, for the emotional thing anyway.

JIM: So you just got a little tipsy and slept with this guy?

JAN: Yeah. Right! I never got rip-roaring drunk or anything. Just mellow. And flirtatious. The whole thing was like poured, focused on flirtatiousness and the whole thing that I was doing. [. . .]

JIM: So it didn't . . . The first time that you slept . . . how did you feel after that?

JAN: No way at all, really, just like, well, I had already, I mean I wasn't a virgin.

JIM: Were you really impressed with yourself that you had earned a hundred dollars in just a short time?

JAN: Yeah, I was.

JIM: Just by sleeping with some dude?

JAN: Yeah, I wasn't jumping for joy or anything, but I was just thinking, "Hm." Well, here's part of it. Oh, right. Oh, the thing is, that night, I think that very night, and this is what I said, I made the whole three hundred that night with just three guys. And so then I was really glad, and I felt very kind of smug and like the cat's pajamas or something, and thinking, "Wow, I made the whole money for John in just a night." And I saw no reason to stop there. And I thought, "Well, this is the easiest, best, most fun job I've ever had, so why don't I just keep doing it?''

JIM: So, how often . . . How much money did you start to make then?

JAN: Well, it wasn't always, you know, it just turned out that it was easy and I managed to do that three-hundred-dollar thing that night. Sort of almost like beginner's luck.

JIM: Right.

JAN: Because then later it would be like some guy would sort of balk at a hundred and say, "Well, how about fifty?" And I'd say, "OK," you know. And so there were various different denominations. But I didn't really get completely sick of it until I'd been in Phoenix for three months doing it. And also working in a massage parlor, too.

JIM: Working in that place called the Samoan Club?

JAN: Well, it was the Samoan Village Hotel. It's probably still there. On Van Buren. That was it. On Van Buren Avenue. And it was a . . . It had a Samoan decor. It's like it had all that tropical stuff, you know. And it was just for tourists, basically, but on top of that they had a little sort of business on the side, you know. Which I guess maybe a lot of . . . Now that I think about it, I bet a lot of places have that going on, and you just don't know it.

JIM: Motels and hotels?

JAN: Yeah, because they're just sort of sleazeball operations.

JIM: They're just providing a service for their customers.

JAN: Or not necessarily their customers at the hotel. Well, maybe. At that place, that's true. That was what we did, we, uh, went, we'd get a key from somebody, and we'd go to the . . . Just pay . . . . What did we do? I can't really remember the details, but we got busted. And the cops raided it.

JIM: You describe that in *Baby Driver*. What are some of the bad things that you remember about being a prostitute?

JAN: Oh. Well. The individual experiences, each one of those is not necessarily very bad, but cumulatively, over time, the constant experience, over and over again, of sleeping with some guy that you don't know for the money is wearing. It wears on you. [. . .] And also, well, also the dynamic of thinking that you need some kind of drug or alcohol to mask the feeling or sort of blot out disgust or feelings of revulsion or whatever, because I mean, you can't really, truly be attracted to all these guys. It's obviously an industry.

JIM: And there must have been some pretty nasty-looking guys.

JAN: Weird-looking guys. Yeah. Big fat guys. There were some of those. Some of them didn't smell very good, and you know, after a while you think, "Oh boy, what am I doing? This is kind of disgusting." Then again, sometimes there's some nice-looking guys, but at that point you're sort of hardened. You don't care what they look like, because you know that you're just doing it for money. And so it creates this kind of attitude in your head, this mercenary attitude of "I sleep with guys for money." You know, which at first might be, you know, bolster you up in some kind of egotistic way of thinking, "Well aren't I really slick and smart 'cause I know how to make money off these guys?" But then after a while it wears on you. You start feeling . . . You realize the tables are really turned, and you're really abusing yourself or allowing yourself to be abused in a funny way for money. I mean, you think you're in control, but actually somehow working against you. Because really, if you take it to the limit, and you just become a prostitute all your life, you become just an insensitive old bag. And that would never be good. Oh, supposedly the reason I reasoned in my mind for why I was stopping at the time was that I didn't want to ruin my feelings. I didn't want to numb . . . 'cause I felt this numbness starting to take over, of like "OK, here we go again. All right, all right. Another hundred dollars."

JIM: But you're earning that money by being totally intimate with somebody that you don't even know.

JAN: I know! But you get into a routine where it's sort of like making the hundredth hamburger, you know. It's not . . . you don't really feel anything. You act out a bunch of attitudinal feelings, I mean, playacted sort of feelings. But you don't really feel them.

JIM: Presumably you had a boyfriend at the same time you were being a prostitute, right?

JAN: At first I didn't, and then later, for a while, I did, but it was also the boyfriend of my madam. And she . . .

JIM: The Indian woman [in *Baby Driver*]?

JAN: Yeah. Jenny . . . . Oh, I know what it really was: Jetty. Well, we don't want anyone to know this, 'cause she could probably come after me and murder me. Jetty Red Elk. That was her real name. And she was very . . .

JIM: You call her Jenny Red Deer in the novel.

JAN: Yeah, because I didn't want to give the real name, because you know, that's the underworld, I mean the crime world.

JIM: No book is worth dying for, as Ed Sanders says.

JAN: Yeah. And that would be sort of like being one of the girls of Heidi Fleiss or something, and then writing a book about the madam's name. I don't know. But anyway . . .

JIM: But anyway, you were just about to say you were going through this reasoning process to get yourself to quit, and that it was because you started to get numb.

JAN: Yeah. And I even thought to myself and would say to myself out loud, "I don't want to be numb like this always. I might fall in love with somebody, and I would miss out on a real true feeling for someone if I keep doing this, because it's numbing me." And so I . . . And after . . . Well, that's not all that happened there, though, because I was drinking way too much, and somehow or other, the combination of drinking way too much and doing that also . . . What happened? I'm trying to remember. I think it was . . . Something happened. I went to the hospital. Oh, that was the first time that I had high blood pressure!

JIM: No kidding. It was 1972 when you first started?

JAN: Yeah. It was like a short episode of extremely high blood pressure that was discovered, and then I was released. And nobody knew why.

JIM: That was when you went to the hospital?

JAN: No, that was when I went to the Maricopa County Hospital in Phoenix.

JIM: Oh, in Phoenix. OK.

JAN: And at that point, I was so young and stupid and crazy that I went in . . . I had no idea what was going on or whether it was serious or not, and I didn't really care, because I was just this drunken floozie most of the time. So I went in and I remember looking out the fourth-story window of the hospital towards New Mexico, seeing these far-off hills and saying, "Hey, I've got to get out of here. I'm going back to New Mexico." Plus, I had this wonderful car then. I had that '61 Eldorado Cadillac convertible.

JIM: That you got from . . . ?

JAN: That guy, Dewey. Walter Dewey White.

JIM: Oh, right. The truck driver.

JAN: He was a short guy, but he was really macho, and the weird thing was I was playing a game, sort of hide-and-go-seek, with my madam, who also . . . We liked each other a lot, too, and in fact, that almost approached lesbianism, because there was a certain thing that lots of guys would ask for, which was a . . . What did they call it? A show? Oh, right. They wanted two women. They'd pay more for this. [. . .] Two women, and it would be me and her. I mean, she and I. [. . .] We agreed to do this a lot, because we just felt really easy with each other, you know, and it didn't really matter. So we'd do a fake kind of show for them, what we imagined that women do together, but it wasn't really real. It was just for the guy, because then he would pay more. And so we did this several times a day.

JIM: So the guy is just basically watching you two make love to each other?

JAN: Yeah, except it's a show. It's not really real. Uh, and also that required being drunk, because, you know, I mean if you were just dead sober, it would just be too much.

JIM: Too weird?

JAN: Too weird, yeah, and too close and too . . . A lot of things. Uh, but when you've got that veneer of alcohol in your brain it's just like nothing really touches you. That's why I understand this whole thing about my father, because I know that, like, when he saw me, he had this fear in his eyes. He didn't want to have this big emotional confrontation, like "My daughter, come here," you know, and all. He wasn't capable of that, and maybe that's what gave me the idea of using alcohol to shield myself against feelings. Yeah, and uh . . . Well, anyway. So then I also, when I was up in that hospital . . .

JIM: You were saying you were playing a game of hide-and-seek with your madam.

JAN: Oh, right! Because I didn't think — well, this is funny — because I didn't think she knew about Dewey. I didn't think she knew I . . . Well, I think he was her husband. And I was having this affair, so I was actually doing this behind her back, but I think it turned out in the end that she had known all along. I can't remember, though.

JIM: So you were having sex with her for your clients, having an affair with her husband, and then you had a boyfriend at the same time.

JAN: [laughs] I know, it's really terrible. It's really bad, bad, bad. Well, he was the boyfriend. He was the only boyfriend. Plus, I was staying at this little dump called the Golden West Motel, but I have that in *Baby Driver*. That was really the name.

JIM: You had a step van named Fred?

JAN: No, that was later. See, that was a different trip. Carol and I went back in '73. And my idea was that . . .

JIM: So you went to Phoenix by yourself that summer?

JAN: The first time, yeah.

JIM: How did you make that connection at the Samoan Club?

JAN: Well, there was some guy that I met at the Forge who said, "Hey, why don't you come out to Phoenix. I got a great situation for you." Like he was an entrepreneurial kind of pimp or something. I don't remember exactly what he got out of the whole thing, but . . . And also it was so hot in Phoenix, it was just like being under the sun's anvil. In the three months that I was there you couldn't even go outside, really, without dying after five minutes of exposure. So I don't know. The whole thing was so intense, with all the drinking and all the . . . and pills. We were taking, like I mention in *Baby Driver*, there was a certain combination, a drink that we made, Jetty and I, for the perfect effect, which sounds really trashy, too.

JIM: I was disgusted by that.

JAN: It is trashy, I know. I wouldn't touch it now.

JIM: What was it again? I don't remember.

JAN: Spañada wine . . .

JIM: Oh God, that's bad enough by itself.

JAN: And Squirt and crushed ice. And with that we would take [in a Southern accent] white crosses or bennies. And that was a sort of a goofball. It was like the alcohol, but the upper of the bennies, so then we were in the perfect . . . It was like a work drug. I mean a work cocktail.

JIM: Primitive Prozac.

JAN: Yeah, well, it was so easy to drink. It was like Kool-Aid. We'd just sort of drink it and drink it all day long in this trailer thing. It was really trashy.

JIM: But that was a massage parlor?

JAN: Yeah. Most of the time these out-of-shape guys would come in and want a massage, and then some other "thing," unmentionable thing, um, and that was par for the course. But every once in a while there'd be this young, really in-shape guy, all tanned, who had been some workman outside, you know, but young and really firm and everything, and a few of these guys didn't even want to take their shorts off.

JIM: They actually wanted a massage?

JAN: They really did.

JIM: To kind of let down after the day's work?

JAN: Yeah, and that was what got me thinking. I thought, "Wow!" You know, and I was attracted to some of them. I thought, "Well, this is a really neat guy." Well, just physically, you know, I couldn't get to know him. But I thought, "You know, that would be really sad if I continued to do this and got more and more, like, numbed about any sort of romantic thing." Because at that point, I was immune to any kind of romantic thing, because I was just in this cycle of work.

JIM: Business is business.

JAN: And also I had so much money I didn't know what to do with it. Cash, cash coming out of my ears. Stacks and stacks of it. And I wasn't saving for anything in particular. And so I'd go — There was that one scene [in *Baby Driver*] that I wrote where I went back to the Golden West Motel in my drugged-up alcohol stupor and counted up all this money that I had made in one week, and it was like stacks of hundreds, stacks of fifties, stacks of twenties, stacks of tens, and I was actually sick of handling the money. It was like, ugh! Like a sickening substance, really. And I knew that I had unlimited ability for making more and more and more of it, if I just stayed there. But I had no idea what I even wanted at that point in my life. And I actually sat there on the bed and looked at all the money, and I just said, "Ugh! I don't want any more of this." You know, I actually wanted to just throw it. I was just throwing it, you know, and it was just, "What am I doing with all this stuff?" But then the hospital thing happened, and as I was up on the fourth floor looking over east toward New Mexico and seeing those blue mountain ranges, I thought, "Hey, I want to go back to Santa Fe." All of a sudden. And see my friends. 'Cause I had been completely estranged from the friends I had made there, you know. And also I thought, "Hey, yeah, I can go back and I'll be like this heroine." Sort of like, "Oh, look what I've done. Look what I've gone and done all by myself, and I've got all this money." Like some big swashbuckler again. So that appealed to me and I thought . . .

JIM: The prostitute as pirate.

JAN: Uh, something. Anyway. And also, I thought, "Hey, I could be just like my mother. My mother had always told me this story. She had been in some hospital, when she was younger, for something — I forgot what — and she had decided to just walk out. And she had made all the doctors very angry, and she was very independent. And I thought, "Yeah, that's what I'll do. I'll just walk out like my mother did." You know. And that's what I did. And yet I was probably hurting myself, because they had given me some kind of blood-pressure medication. I just threw it away.

JIM: Mm.

JAN: And so that was my first run-in with high blood pressure, and I didn't know it was going to be continuous. I didn't even really care at that point, because I was so crazy and young. You know. So I actually went out to the parking lot. I just walked out and I just drove in my Cadillac. And I drove all the way to New Mexico.

JIM: And is that the time, or was it the previous summer, when the tires started to go bad, and you stop and have sex with some dude in a gas station for a new set of tires?

JAN: Wait a minute!

JIM: That's in *Baby Driver*.

JAN: Oh, now I remember that. Wow! That's funny. I'd really totally forgotten. That was in Holbrook. Holbrook, Arizona. That's right. I don't know what had happened exactly. I guess I did need new tires, 'cause that's right, they were bald. That's the term. And, uh, this was a young guy, too. He was just a mechanic. And somehow or other we made this deal. Maybe he did this all the time. You know, a lot of people came through there, you know, needing things done to their cars. And I guess if he saw a good-looking woman who needed something done, then he would just offer her this deal, and of course it was a perfect deal for me, 'cause I was in the same kind of thing. So we did that. And then I took off again.

JIM: Yeah. Did any of the people you slept with when you were a prostitute do things to you that scared you, or like did any of them get violent on you?

JAN: No. And that's a funny thing that I wonder about sometimes, that I was gonna tell you about the other night, too: I've never been battered. Ever. I've been with hundreds of guys in all kinds of situations like that, and also just a boyfriend or whatever, and the closest I ever came to being hit was the time when Michael Hagberg [the model for the character Bruce in *Trainsong*] — Well, he wasn't hitting me, though. He was hitting the window and other things, but, uh . . .

JIM: He sort of picked you up and threw you on the bed or something, didn't he?

JAN: That's true. OK. That's probably closer then. That's true.

JIM: That's pretty close.

JAN: Yeah, but he was . . . Yeah. But it wasn't a constant thing. It was just that one thing. And also the time when I had told Michael Hagberg when we were living in Spokane, "Don't ever hit me." And he said, "Oh no, of course not, baby." But then that day, when he was trying to impress his friend, he took like a dishtowel off the refrigerator and swatted me in the face. And then I got really furious after he left, and I just left, and I never saw him again. I said, "Well, that'll teach him."

JIM: So nobody ever got violent, but did they make demands on you that you thought were just totally inappropriate?

JAN: Well, see, I was always in control, so I never allowed that to happen. I would say, "No, I won't do that. Or I'll do this and this, but I won't do that." Or whatever. And they never, well, they never tried anything because they knew they were in this establishment and there were lots of — I guess there were just girls out there, but I guess we could have all have jumped them or done something. I don't know what they thought, but they never did try that. Nobody ever did.

JIM: Can I ask you where you drew the line?

JAN: Oh. Uh, let's see. Let's see, where did I draw the line? It depended on the situation. Uh . . .

JIM: You mean how drunk you were?

JAN: Or what the guy was like, or . . . I didn't really like to do blow jobs, particularly. Um, in fact, at a certain point I decided I wouldn't. Like, "I don't do windows," you know. And I don't do windows, you know. OK.

JIM: That's just not on the list of options.

JAN: Well, not for a bunch of guys that I don't know, but of course with my boyfriends it would be different. But I just decided . . . And then little by little, I kept drawing more lines. And then pretty soon I just didn't want to do anything anymore. And so I stopped.

JIM: So you sort of eased your way out of it by being stricter and stricter.

JAN: Yeah. So. And then I . . .

JIM: Any sort of aftereffects that you notice over the years from having done that?

JAN: Well, actually, I've actually even heard that this — what happened to me with the kidney failure — is not that uncommon for women who have done that. Because — I don't know if this is true, but it might be — that actually, you know, the constant pressure against your, I mean, through here [gestures to her pelvis] but into your back, plus drinking a lot at the same time, can really wear out your kidneys. And that makes sense. But it was only three months. But that was enough for me, maybe. So. And also, it's not just the physical aspect, it's probably the whole psychological aspect, knowing that you're tearing yourself down somehow. Because of course physical things are always sort of psychological and there's really more to everything than we really know.

JIM: And there's always some connection between your mind and your body.

JAN: Yeah.

JIM: Your spirit and your body, for sure.

JAN: And I could — I think I sort of felt that over there. I had a feeling that I better stop. Then again, I mean, if that did the damage right there, then that was enough to make me have kidney failure later on at thirty-nine. Like I didn't know it, but still, maybe it's better I stopped then than continue, 'cause maybe I would have had kidney failure at twenty-five. Who knows?

JIM: Did you ever contract any venereal diseases?

JAN: Uh, I think I had the clap once, but it wasn't during that time, actually.

JIM: You got it from a boyfriend?

JAN: But I didn't really even know about it. It was so fast. It was the second time I came to Phoenix with Carol, and I sort of felt like I was corrupting my friend, my best friend. [. . .] Maybe I should go in sequence, so I can say where I was living and all that, if you want to know. It sort of gets all garbled up.

JIM: Well, I'm more interested about the topic of prostitution.

JAN: Oh, OK. You pervert! [laughs]

JIM: I know. It's not just me, though. It's the whole society. You know, you watch, if this ends up in the book . . .

JAN: You mean in your book?

JIM: Yeah. And we have to go and talk to people on talk shows, that's the first thing they'll want to know.

JAN: Sure, they'll want to know all about it. That's all they'll want to know. That's true. I mean, well, I know that. I know that women, when they know that I've done that, are always amazed that I did that.

JIM: Fascinated, though?

JAN: Fascinated, yeah.

JIM: Do they want you to tell them the details?

JAN: Well, not — Most women won't even admit that they're interested enough to want to know about it, but they are. I can tell that they are. And most men are afraid to admit it, too, in a different way. So . . .

JIM: Why?

JAN: Just regular people. Well, they think they're being too invasive to ask you questions like that. Like that they're going to ruin your friendship or something. Or that they're gonna look like an asshole or something.

JIM: But everybody's curious about everybody else's sex life.

JAN: Sure, but they're afraid to ask, usually. Unless they have a real good premise, like being an interviewer or something, you know. A reason for it.

JIM: Yeah, OK. It's a great excuse to ask the unaskable questions.

JAN: Oh, wouldn't it be great to have Mike Wallace . . .

JIM: Oh, he'd be right in your face, accusing you of corrupting the youth of Phoenix or something.

JAN: He'd probably talk to you in the third person. He'd say, "Now how does Jan feel about this?"

JIM: Right, right, right.

JAN: I'd say, "Whattya mean?"

JIM: [imitating Mike Wallace] You say you were totally without scruples?

JAN: That's right. That's right, Mike. I was. You hit the nail on the head. Well, anyway.

JIM: Is there any connection — I don't want this to sound wrong — is there any connection between being a prostitute and having slept with so many men as boyfriends?

JAN: Probably.

JIM: You just used the figure "hundreds," and so — Although, back to the baby-boomer topic, I think for people growing up in the so-called sexual revolution, I don't think it's that unusual. People who've slept with tens or hundreds of partners.

JAN: Especially druggies.

JIM: And boozers.

JAN: Yeah. And also, but, people from a one-parent family. It's more likely that that would happen, because that cuts down your morals. I mean your foundation for being a good girl or a good boy or whatever. [. . .]

JIM: Did the fact that you were able to be a prostitute have a connection to the fact that you had so many lovers?

JAN: Oh. Later on, I think it probably, it was probably the same reason, basically, I mean the same psychological reason for both things, that I was looking for a father. That's what everyone tells me, and it seems to make sense to me that having a big, absent zero instead of a father . . . But then it's also another thing, because it wasn't just any father. It was a very special guy, who a lot of people loved and revered, or at least idolized, but I didn't know him. Only all these other people knew him. I don't know exactly what effect — I mean I can't quite verbalize what effect that really had on me, 'cause I don't really know, but I know that it must have had an effect on me.

JIM: Well, their relationship is similar to the prostitute's relationship with a client.

JAN: Right.

JIM: It's somebody that everybody else respects. Like you were sleeping with politicians in the state of New Mexico. Public figures.

JAN: And I was actually proud of myself for coming to New Mexico alone — well, I wasn't really — I mean winding up in New Mexico totally alone, fending for myself and working as a waitress, and then sort of switching over to being with these big, important guys, you know. And I thought, "Well, I can, I can make it on my own. Look at me." You know. And I had the same feeling about my mother, although she would never have done that. She had morals and principles, but she didn't think she had to put them on me. She thought that I would naturally have them, because she thought so highly of me that she always had assumed that I would just know intrinsically what was right and wrong. But she was wrong about that, as it turned out.

JIM: How could she have taught, how could she have taught you her values?

JAN: Well, a lot of parents try.

JIM: But it doesn't seem like your personality was such that you have accepted her authority.

JAN: No, I was too rebellious. Well, she did tell me a few times, you know, what was right and wrong, and I shouldn't do this and shouldn't do that, but I wouldn't listen to her. That's just the way I was.

JIM: So now, any, still any lingering residue about your — like something equivalent to your hallucination, your constant hallucinations — about having been a prostitute?

JAN: I don't even think about it anymore. Most of the time. I mean unless there's some reason for talking about it or thinking about it. 'Cause I know I'm never gonna do it again.

JIM: Did you ever do it again, later, after this, when you were twenty, twenty-one?

JAN: I think I probably did, but I can't remember exactly when. Uh, hm, that'd be something to think about. I mean I always knew I had the capability after that, but I wasn't really that interested in doing it. [. . .]

JIM: But weren't you ever tempted, you know, to turn back to prostitution just because you knew that you had done it, you could do it again, and it was an easy way to make some money fast.

JAN: Hm. Yeah, I might have had that in the back of my mind, but once I stopped at that time, I really didn't want to do it again for a lot of reasons. Also, when you're in a stable place, and you're in one place, it's much better to do it in that situation, where you've at least got your protection, and you've got a place, and all that, but if you're actually out on your own, traveling, along a long stream like North to South America, that could haunt you. That could have all kinds of bad repercussions, like you could wind up in some horrible Mexican jail. Anything could happen. I guess I just knew that, plus I didn't really — I wasn't really thinking about — I was into the romantic thing then, see, which was the thing I wanted to keep fresh. And that's the reason I quit in the first place. And I don't know, at that point I was more into doing things like making jewelry, speaking Spanish. I don't know what I — It's really hard to psychoanalyze myself, looking back at all the details and things, but I'm trying, in general at least, to explain how I felt. [. . .]

JIM: Did being a stripper bear any resemblance to being a hooker?

JAN: Kind of. In fact, most of the strippers actually had the hooking thing on the side. But at that point I wasn't interested in that anymore. I just wanted to do the dancing. There's so many different combinations of it, you know. [. . .]

JIM: Maybe this is a dopey question, but is the fact that you have been a prostitute and a stripper and even a go-go dancer, are those really like, are those valuable experiences in your life?

JAN: Oh, well, they're just things that happened, and so I don't know if they're valuable or not. They're just there. Like I wouldn't — Well, if I had it to do over again now and I had my head screwed on straight, I wouldn't do it now, because I know that it was really bad for me. Well, I wouldn't drink, either, that is. But then again I don't know, in a parallel universe, if I had enough chance, I might turn out to just be a person who is prone to drinking again anyway. So I don't even know if I would have power over myself to say, "I'm not gonna drink this time." [. . .]

JIM: I just have one more question.

JAN: Oh.

JIM: Did being a prostitute or being a stripper give you a sense of power over men? Because I think that's something that a lot of people in those professions describe.

JAN: Yeah, it did. And yet I guess I was sharp enough to realize that if I kept it up, they would have started to have power over me instead.

JIM: How so?

JAN: Well, 'cause the whole thing is kind of abusive. You're allowing yourself to be physically and emotionally abused — and sexually. Uh, and supposedly the big prize is money, yet meanwhile, you're tearing yourself down and ruining your life, really, by doing this. So what? Big whoop. Tons of money. You know, I just realized that.

JIM: Is there a way to do it without damage — like we talked about the situation in Amsterdam? Is there a way to do it so that it doesn't damage the woman so much?

JAN: I bet in Amsterdam with a program like that, well, I'm sure it would be better, but I bet it still would tear you down psychologically. I'm sure it would, because basically it's still the same dynamic of man after man after man. It's not normal. It's not natural, you know. It's because of money. Well, then again, it's the oldest — supposedly the oldest, second oldest occupation in the world, so it's been going on for a long time, so that in itself might make it natural.

JIM: Well, here's my Mike Wallace thing, too. [Imitating Wallace] It seemed pretty natural for you. A hundred boyfriends by the time you were fourteen.

JAN: Hm. True. I guess I already had a propensity for it even then. It was because of my father not being there.

JIM: Well, here's the other issue, too, that's involved with that.

A lot of — I've read that a lot of prostitutes are frigid, or that they don't enjoy having sex.

JAN: Yeah. That was me, too.

JIM: Yeah?

JAN: Then, that changed later. And luckily, 'cause that's the whole reason I did consciously decide to change it, and then I was right, as it turns out, because in the beginning when I was just sort of — I was already kind of numb in a way that I didn't really feel much.

JIM: You mean from having all the boyfriends?

JAN: No, just because of the way I was. Just because that's the way I was. And then . . .

JIM: Not — sort of — like your mother describes feeling like her neurons were disconnected?

JAN: Well, it was different for my mother. I don't know. I never quite figured out . . . [. . .] You know what I think? Well, maybe I'm wrong. Maybe there are a lot of young girls who really do feel a lot, you know, and go nuts and all that. But, well, in my case, when I was younger, I just didn't have — I mean it took a long time for all the neurons to be activated. You know, a whole lifetime of things, you know, until you become a mature woman and you really start feeling everything. But maybe that's not always the case with every woman. I don't know, 'cause I can't say. But that's how it was with me. Like at first it was just like a little show, flirtation and then going through the motions, and ha ha ha, you know, whatever. [. . .] I never actually felt horny, completely horny, and wanted a man for that. I never felt that until way later. In fact, until Carter [her boyfriend in Eugene, Oregon, in 1989]. That was the thing. Carter — there was this thing with him that was just really wild, you know.

JIM: So you were nearly forty by the time you felt some kind of intense desire?

JAN: Well, I was thirty-eight or something. Thirty-eight, thirty-seven. Something like that. [Jan gives a brief history of her sexual life, including the first onset of her period, her eight pregnancies, and a serious infection of her reproductive organs discovered only in the late 1980s.]

JIM: Your reproductive system has taken some abuse.

JAN: Who knows, maybe that [infection] happened when I was doing the bad thing. Huh, huh. You know. [. . .] But now I could care less about sex. In fact, sex would annoy me now, because I have this itching problem everywhere on my body, and so I've noticed even if I go and have a massage, I wind up in a paroxysm of itching, because the masseuse invariably touches me too lightly. Like I want to be touched really hard. [. . .]

JIM: So there's nothing about sex or having a boyfriend that you miss?

JAN: Only the companionship. But I also know that if I had the companionship with one person for a long period of time, the dynamic between the two people invariably shifts. And I know how that happens, because it's happened so many times before. And I almost don't want to go through that psychodrama anymore. I like to be a friend but have the detachment, so that you can just be free to be a friend without any possessive feelings or anything. That seems to be what sex does: just causes you to have these feelings of possessiveness. And that destroys everything, every time, because it's not possible to carry on a friendship with that going on too, 'cause then you can't let the other person live his life — his or her life — without flying into a rage or something. One person always flies into a rage, and the other one becomes independent and rebellious and says, "I can do anything I want." And it's either me or the other person that does that. And it's like I've been through that so many times, why bother anymore? It's just, forget it, you know? I'd rather have friends. That's how I feel about it. Plus, I can't afford to be contaminated by anyone else's fluids, since I'm so vulnerable to infection.

EIGHT

IN AND OUT OF MARRIAGE

The first year and a half of the new decade — the 1970s — were trying months for Jan. Like many a city hippie, she never quite got used to life in the country. The small state university in Ellensburg generated only a minimal subculture, but at least it was something, and Jan and John made the best of it, making friends easily in that era of revolutionary fervor. John continued to develop his interest in Asian religions and astrology, while Jan practiced her jewelry-making. John picked up seasonal agricultural jobs, and Jan eventually went to work in the local food co-op, the first job she had ever held for more than a few weeks. They tried to accept or ignore Joan's irrational behavior, though they found it a bit difficult when she took out the toilet in her cabin in Kittitas, a small bedroom community just a few miles east of Ellensburg, where the young couple had settled next door. Jan's half-brother, David, who was only about ten at the time, seemed not to mind at all, keeping himself occupied with childish experiments in his bedroom.

When Jan turned eighteen in the winter of 1970, she must have wondered to herself how she could have come so far and experienced so much in just a few short years. As she sipped coffee with her mother around the woodstove, their thoughts turned together to Jack. It began to work on Jan that she would never see him again. She was as far from New York City here as she had been in the jungle of Mexico, and the two deaths — her child's and her father's — began to separate her from her own childhood.

John hastened her growing up as well, when he began to fool around with Jenny, one of the young girls in his astrology group. Let it be said that in the spirit of the times he did this quite openly, explaining to Jan in hippie cant that they should share themselves with other people. She was bewildered by her own jealousy, having never loved a man as she loved John, and many years later, she still could not explain how or why they split up. As her barely fictionalized version of events in *Baby Driver* attests, however, she took John at his word, and when his best friend Hilaire Hiler, the son of a Left Bank expatriate artist, arrived from South America, Jan took them both to bed with her. Their ménage à trois only made Jan's marital status more confusing, and she resolved to make some kind of drastic move.

Hilaire's sister, Nicole (or Deedee, as she was called in real life), was living at the time in a small town near Santa Fe, and the more he talked about the Southwest, the more excited Jan became about seeing it. Bright blue skies sounded better than Washington snow and rain, but still Jan was reluctant to leave her husband behind. Finally, she cajoled John into joining her on the trek south, but when the time came to book the flight, he backed out, pleading that he wanted to finish the book he was writing. So Jan and Hilaire boarded the bus to Seattle without John. In *Baby Driver* Jan imagines John looking up regretfully from his typewriter as her jet wings over their little house on its way to Albuquerque. Although it didn't happen quite that romantically, John did follow Jan to the Southwest, but she had hit the ground running, and by the time he arrived, she had already established a new way of life for herself.

An important aspect of this new way of life was work, something Jan had done only fitfully heretofore. Thanks to a false start as a barmaid at a place called Frank's Lounge, Jan suddenly found herself in possession of a black 1955 Cadillac, which Frank had intended to give with strings attached. But Jan played dumb, using her new vehicle first to escape, then to look for a new job. By virtue of the proverbial smallness of the world, she soon found one. A young woman named Peggy Bull, a horsewoman, had also recently moved down from Ellensburg. Jan ran into town to tell Peggy her troubles, and Peggy got her a job cleaning stables at Santa Fe Downs racetrack. Jan was thrilled, and this job somehow gave her a new impetus to write.

A little stoned "Jabberwocky" imitation gave her the first title for her novel-to-be: "while everthreads sag à la mode adobe."

She would call the book — if she ever finished it — *Everthreads*. Though the title was replaced ten years later by one suggested by her editor, an image from that period got into *Baby Driver*, one Jan scrawled on a piece of notepaper one morning as she worked in the stalls: "I rolled out of lavender nylon sheets, stuck my feet into shit encrusted cowboy boots, and jumped into my old black Cadillac." Maybe this association caused her to remember the job fondly, but whatever the case, she carried her photo ID from the racetrack for years, and she was devastated when she finally lost it.

About this time she also had an affair with a local boy her age named Antonio, who introduced her to the native hangouts in Tesuque, as well as to the street scene in southwest Albuquerque. Jan also continued to sleep with Hilaire in a rather desultory way, and when Nicole's husband arrived from the Middle East, Jan had a fling with him as well. In *Baby Driver*, Deedee gets so angry about this combined breach of fidelity and hospitality that she shoots her husband. Just as Jack Kerouac's acquaintances served him in his writing, many of Jan's new friends now became the basis for characters in *Baby Driver*, including John's sister, Deborah, who joined Jan in New Mexico and remained a lifelong friend. Drugs were abundant, and Jan, perhaps because her jobs tended to be in bars, also began to drink heavily for the first time. Later she would blame her alcoholism for her failure to inquire into rights in her father's estate at the time. After Jan visited him briefly in Ellensburg in 1972, John decided to join her in Santa Fe, which became his base of operations as a writer for many years.

Though John and Jan set up housekeeping together once again, it was clear to both of them that their separation had created a permanent rift in their relationship. Even though they continued to love each other deeply, neither was satisfied with marriage. They brought other lovers home and slept with them in separate bedrooms. Occasionally, the tension got the better of them, as for instance, when John one day hurled a hamburger against the kitchen wall in a fit of jealous pique. Still they struggled to stay together. John's relocated astrology classes provided him with plenty of opportunities to meet new women, though they failed to provide much income.

One day, sometime after her twentieth birthday, Jan did have a windfall, though it turned out to be a rather fateful one. A man dressed in a suit knocked at the door, and when Jan opened it, he introduced himself as an official of the Florida court, a guardian ad litem, assigned to protect Jan's interest in her father's estate. If Jan would sign a few papers, he would give her $500, which seemed to her like a huge sum at the time. Otherwise, she could hire a lawyer and fight the settlement, but that would cost money she didn't have. Unthinking, she jumped at the chance, using the name Janet Michele Aly, thus signing away her rights in her father's meager estate, which consisted mainly of the house he and his mother and Stella were living in when he died. (Court documents specify the actual consideration for Jan's signature on a quit-claim deed as only $10, but Jan recalled the much larger sum.)

Soon, the money had disappeared, and Jan began to cast about for ways to support herself and John without having to spend so much time working menial jobs. One night, one of her male drinking buddies gave her a tip. Get yourself all dressed up, he advised, go down to the Forge (a Santa Fe nightspot near the state capitol), and wait at the bar for a proposition. Proposition? The word didn't register at first. Then it dawned on Jan what the guy was suggesting, and instead of being offended, she asked herself, Why not? Of course, she wouldn't have to tell John where the money was coming from, even though she persisted in thinking that she was doing it for him. So one Friday night after the state legislature had convened, Jan dolled herself up in a slinky red dress she had purchased specially for her new career, walked south across the plaza down to the Forge, sat down at the bar, ordered a drink, and waited.

She didn't have to wait long, because soon a lonely politician from a distant corner of the state sauntered over and sat down beside her. After a couple more drinks, Jan became flirtatious, and the man suggested they "go somewhere." Somewhere turned out to be his hotel room, and almost before she knew it, Jan had turned her first trick. Kindly, perhaps, that first john explained the protocol of payment. He would leave his money on the dresser, and when Jan got up to get dressed, she could pick it up without actually taking it from him. Technically, she supposed, that made it legal. She took her first $100 — she could hardly believe anyone would pay her so much for sex — and returned to the Forge, where she eventually met two more clients that same evening. Late the next morning, as she began to stir in her own bed, Jan savored the thought that she had earned $300 without lifting a finger. She felt as though she had pulled one over on her johns.

Of course, as she quickly discovered, not only did she not earn $300 every night, but there were also obvious drawbacks to her new line of work. Not all the guys were all that appealing, though some were, and almost all of them were somewhat paranoid and secretive. One fellow, destined to become a powerful New Mexico politician, picked Jan up in a brown Cadillac, took her to a motel, then stood by the window watching to make sure no one was spying on him. One night at the Forge, an older prostitute she had met during the first few weeks of hooking turned Jan on to a golden opportunity. Some aging oil millionaire needed a companion for an evening, and if Jan would simply drive down to Albuquerque, she could make $500 in a single night. She did so somewhat apprehensively, fearing that the old geezer might be some sort of pervert, but it turned out that he wasn't even interested in sex. Jan merely had to spend the night in his bed, and in the morning on her way to breakfast, one of the hotel employees slipped her an envelope containing the cash.

A few months passed, and Jan began to grow weary of the routine. Drinking in the Forge one night with the same guy who had made the original suggestion that she sell herself for sex, she took another tip from him. Apparently, he had some sort of professional connections with the management of a bar and motel in Phoenix called the Samoan Village Hotel, which sported a tropical island decor and served its customers more than eats and sheets. Braving the summer heat of the Arizona desert, she took her black Cadillac on the road, with only the name of a contact in Phoenix. This turned out to be Jetty Red Elk, the Native American madam of the Samoan Village Hotel on Van Buren Street. She hired Jan on the recommendation of her friend in Santa Fe, started her on the job, and introduced her to her husband, one Walter Dewey White, whom Jan described as a truck driver with a "white trash country Western mentality." Soon she was turning tricks with the snowbirds at the motel, performing simulated lesbian sex with Jetty for the customers for extra cash, and having an affair with Walter on the side. With the daily drinking and the tension caused by the threat of possible police raids, alcohol now became an integral part of Jan's life, as one may well imagine.

When fall came, however, Jan began to miss her friends in Santa Fe, and without much ado she loaded up Matilda, the 1961 Eldorado Dewey had given her to replace the '55 Caddy Frank had unwittingly donated, which had died, and headed back north. When she started having trouble controlling the car near Holbrook, Arizona, a service station attendant told her that her tires were completely bald and intimated to Jan that he would replace them in exchange for certain services rendered. Given her recent occupation, Jan readily agreed, and with Matilda newly shod, she drove the rest of the way back to Santa Fe.

Jan got back to New Mexico in time for the 1972 presidential election, and several nights before Nixon's landslide she got into an argument with a McGovern supporter in a Santa Fe bar. Having paid no attention to the campaign, she didn't even know who McGovern was, but since she didn't like the guy who supported him, she decided to attack the Democrat. Finally, the argument escalated to the point where Jan set her sights on the man's campaign button, and without warning she leaned over and bit his lapel, ripping the button off and chipping her tooth in the process. It was almost fifteen years before she could afford to have it fixed.

Despite appearances, Jan legally became an adult as of February 16, 1973. She continued to work as a prostitute off and on, but the scene with John was getting weird, and pretty soon she and a new friend, Carol, concocted a plan to go back to Phoenix to work. Matilda, the Eldorado, had died in the meantime, so they loaded up Carol's step van, Henry, and headed south. For Jan it was pretty much a repeat of her last visit, except this time instead of Walter she found a boyfriend her own age, and she and Carol and Jetty concocted a drink made out of Squirt and Spañada wine that kept them in just the right state of inebriation for their nightly labors. Feeling guilty that she was leading her friend astray, Jan eventually found them jobs as go-go dancers. Now they could party every night without having to have sex with strangers.

The drinking and the drugs still counted, though, and that summer of 1973 was marred by Jan's first attack of high blood pressure, for which she had to be hospitalized in the Maricopa County Hospital. Her room there faced east, and Jan looked out the window, fantasizing that she could see the mountains of New Mexico. Later in life she wondered if her few months as a prostitute had contributed to her kidney failure. Most likely, it was her heavy drinking, which even at age 21 might have induced high blood pressure, which is one cause of renal failure. Unbeknownst to Jan, she had also suffered a different kind of loss in 1973: her grandmother, Gabrielle Lévesque Kerouac, still in the care of her daughter-in-law, Stella, had finally succumbed to a series of debilitating strokes. Now Jan became the last of the Kerouacs in her father's line, as her father's last wife inherited the entirety of his nearly worthless estate.

Almost psychically, Jan sensed her new aloneness in the world, and when she returned to Santa Fe she realized that her attachment to John had been some kind of misconceived role-playing. She had been a wild street kid before she met him, and now she felt free to give up her ill-cast character as hippie housewife. She took the first opportunity that presented itself — as usual, in the form of a man. A guy named Ganders was going to Central America, and he invited Jan to join him there. When he cabled her from Nicaragua, she left her past behind again, and without much fanfare began her wildest adventure.

As a preface to Jan's travels in Latin America, you should know that her friend from the racetrack, Peggy Bull, to whom *Baby Driver* is dedicated, had disappeared from Santa Fe without a trace. (She reappeared nearly twenty years later in her hometown of Ellensburg without so much as an explanation of what had happened to her.) In other words, when Jan took off, she knew that it was possible she would never return, but the road was in her blood. The last thing she did before she left was to divorce

John. They went to the county courthouse west of the plaza and filled out the papers together. It cost a dollar in March 1973.

Jan's attempted meeting with Ganders was little more than an excuse to get on the road — in *Baby Driver* she says that when she arrived in Central America she "forgot everything" — so when she missed her connection with him, she wasn't worried. Like her mother, she was fond of the Spanish language, and she moved easily from El Salvador to Nicaragua to Costa Rica. In San José she met an itinerant jeweler named Miguel, who taught her how to make trinkets for the tourists. Eventually, they made their way further south, first to Ecuador, then to Peru. She spent her twenty-second birthday in Guayaquil. After a narrow escape from Miguel, who had come to believe he was possessed by demons, Jan fell in with a wealthy family in Lima, who took her in. In the space of two days she went from living from hand to mouth to living in the lap of luxury.

While staying with the Zarragoza family, Jan saw another side of life in South America, including some up-close encounters with local coke dealers. Toward the end of March she experienced two major shocks. The first was an earthquake, which Jan, always superstitious, took as an omen that she should return to the States. The second was much more bizarre. As she walked through her neighborhood one day, a tabloid headline captured her attention. "Yankee Tart Disappears in a Puff of Smoke," it screamed. Beneath the headline Jan was astounded to find a photograph of herself. Apparently, Ganders had returned to Santa Fe, misunderstood one of her letters, and reported her missing under the influence of Peggy's disappearance. In a day or two, oddly, a money order from Ganders also arrived. Jan bought a plane ticket, bid farewell to her hosts, and flew to San Diego, as far as she could get on the money. From there she went by bus, not back to Santa Fe, but to Washington State to rejoin her mother and begin her life once again.

Thanks to a brief affair with a local Ellensburg guy who came to Joan's house to buy strawberry plants, Jan soon met the cast of characters that would populate her second novel, *Trainsong*, including the man who became her second husband, the nine-teen-year-old Bernard Hackett. Jan started hanging around at the big house Bernard shared with his fellow New Yorker Malcolm Connover in the Dogtown section of Ellensburg. The continuous party there reminded her of her teenage years in the city, and after she and Bernard started sleeping together regularly, Jan moved her stuff in with the two roomies. During the vegetable harvest the local canning factory, Twin City Foods, hired lots of seasonal workers to process the corn crop. The three new friends all signed on for the night shift, hoping to make enough money in a month to retire for the winter. After partying all evening, the three would change into aprons and rubber boots and walk down to the Twin City plant by the railroad tracks on the west side of Ellensburg. All night long they wrestled ears of corn, fed them into big machines, and cleaned up the waste. By the time the sun came up they were literally sick of the smell. They trudged wearily back to the house, threw their aprons and boots in the bathtub to soak, and turned in for the night. After thirty days none of them ever wanted to see a vegetable again, but they had enough loot to last them through the winter. Jan and Bernard even discussed the possibility of doing some traveling. For his part, Malcolm bought a stack of new jazz albums and a carton of cigarettes and began to settle into his winter routine.

One day, after the weather in the Valley started to turn seriously cold, Jan and Bernard decided to walk out to Kittitas to visit her mother. Midway into the two-hour hike, in the midst of some detailed fantasies about visiting Europe, Bernard sheepishly interrupted Jan by addressing her by her pet name. "Mole," he said, "I've been thinking. You know my father once promised to give me a silver bar he's been saving for me, but there's a condition . . . ." He hesitated to state it, however.

Jan took up the slack. "You have to get married," she guessed.

"Right." Bernard looked at the ground, as though he were ashamed.

"Great!" Jan exclaimed. "Then we'll get married."

It was decided just that quickly and easily, and by the time the affianced couple arrived at the home of the future mother-in-law, they had worked out a plan, which they related excitedly to Joan and David. First they would take the train to New York, heading up to Vancouver and over to Montreal, then back down into the

U.S. At Bernard's parents' home in Queens in October they would get married, and with the silver bar hidden in the clothes in their suitcases, they would sail for Casablanca aboard a freighter. Jan's mother and brother, who had been fantasizing themselves about emigrating to Scotland, agreed it was the most romantic thing they had ever heard.

Providentially, the plan worked, although they altered it slightly by marrying before they left Ellensburg, and on November 13, 1975, they boarded a bus at the Port Authority terminal in Manhattan, rode out to Camden, New Jersey, and settled into a cabin on the Yugoslavian freighter *Tuhobic*, bound for North Africa. According to her account of the journey in *Trainsong*, almost the first thing Jan did after the ship hit the open sea was to have sex with the chief engineer in an empty cabin. Not exactly the perfect way to inaugurate her second marriage, but Jan's way, nevertheless.

One of the other passengers had loaned Jan a paperback book with a picture of a cowboy on the cover, and the first fine morning Jan carried it onto the deck with her to catch some sun. Opening the book without paying any more attention to the cover, she happened on a chapter called "Big Trip to Europe." The book was *Lonesome Traveler* by her father, and the chapter in question described his journey to Tangier in early 1957 aboard a Yugoslavian freighter. Jan suddenly got a feeling of déjà vu. Unconsciously, she was repeating family history. That night she had a dream in which the ship's engineer was throwing overboard several boxes clearly stenciled with the name KEROUAC.

After an unsettling visit to Tangier, Bernard and Jan returned to Casablanca, caught the ferry for Gibraltar, and took a plane from there to London, where they holed up for the winter, living in a meager bedsit in Thornton Heath and stealing milk off doorsteps to supplement their diet. While Bernard hung out at the neighborhood pub, Jan warmed herself by drinking cheap tea and writing about her adventures in Costa Rica three years before. A young waiter at the local Indian restaurant who befriended them was surprised that Jan always wore skirts. One afternoon when she had her Levi's on, she ran into Chadry at the corner market. He exclaimed in a voice loud enough for all the customers to hear,

"I did not recognize you with pants on." Another time, after Bernard explained that Jan was writing a novel, Chadry burst out, "Oh, you are a genius, an ocean of knowledge."

Away from their American friends, Jan began to realize that her relationship with Bernard was based largely on drunken party theatrics. Even their travel had been undertaken as a kind of re-creation of a 1930s movie intrigue. Alone with him for weeks on end in the dingy London winter, she lost interest in her young husband. When the money they got in exchange for the silver bar ran out, the couple flew home to the States, stopping for a couple months with Bernard's brother, Jed, in Queens. While Jan tried to resist having an affair with her brother-in-law, Bernard entertained them both by drawing cartoons of his heart surgeon stepfather, whom he hated. One picture represented the jowly Italian doctor as a human vacuum cleaner, which Bernard dubbed the Egidiclean, playing on the doctor's last name. Jan thought Bernard acted like his brain was on fire.

Amid this chaos Jan recalled her first memories of life in New York City in a brownstone at 200 West 68th Street. As she started to miss her mother, she also began to think of her father, of John Lash, and of her dead baby, Natasha. For some reason, she imagined Jack and her mother living on West 20th Street in 1951. Jack had cranked out the famous scroll version of *On the Road* just before Joan got pregnant with Jan. Jan's mind made the connection between herself and the writer's life. She began to wonder why she was bothering to set down the events of her recent past. Cynically, she was moved to summarize her adventures in Latin America in a single paragraph. Finally, she concluded that no excuse was necessary. In *Trainsong* she set down her thoughts:

> I liked to think that reasons weren't needed at all. I'd always been fond of the notion that things just happened like cards falling or dice clicketing from the random hands of Fate. It was easier that way — no responsibility. And with no dependents, responsibility seemed rather unnecessary.

Visits to her old neighborhood on East 6th Street, however, fueled Jan's desire to capture the past in words, and she continued to work on *Baby Driver* in the face of her lack of a reason for writing.

And despite her growing indifference toward Bernard, the couple returned to the West together. Rather than going back to Ellensburg, they decided to stay in the Seattle area, where they could easily find jobs and some friends who owned an antique store were willing to let them crash in the back room of their shop. While Bernard could only manage a minimum-wage dishwashing gig, Jan landed a position as assistant chef at the Tacoma Ritz Hotel, the first of many restaurant jobs she would work during the next decade. Her boss at the Ritz, one Michael Hagberg, was a big bruiser of a guy, just the type Jan was craving to distance herself further from the wispy Bernard. Michael wasn't bashful either, and the first time Jan bent over to pick up a baked potato, he patted her ass.

Kitchen work, according to Jan, enhances sexuality, and by the end of her first week she was staying after work for free drinks with Michael at the hotel bar. One night during the following week, she went home with him, explaining to Bernard that she didn't relish a long bus ride across town in the wee hours. Bernard failed to take the hint, but when Jan drew her first paycheck, she sent him a less subtle message by renting her own apartment on Pine Street in Tacoma. Before long, Michael had moved in, and Bernard appeared forlornly at their door one afternoon to announce that he was leaving town, going home to New York. Jan hardly recognized him. Without an ounce of regret, she took up her new life with Michael.

Michael, it turned out, had ulterior motives for hooking up with Jan. Within a couple weeks he outlined his new money-making scheme for her: a check-kiting scam. They opened a joint account with $25, and he took Jan out to buy her an expensive suit of clothes. Dressed now as a well-heeled young lady, she proceeded to purchase item after item at all the best Seattle-area stores, returning the following day to exchange the goods she bought with hot checks for cash. It seemed like a breeze. Predictably, however, she and Michael got greedy, and in January 1977 they found the police waiting at the door of a department store after one of Jan's visits. They both landed in the Tacoma jail.

Apparently, Michael was a fast talker, because Jan was surprised when she was soon summoned from her holding cell to appear before a magistrate, who released her on her own recognizance. Michael had promised the police chief that he could lead him to a local heroin dealer if he and his girlfriend were both sprung from jail. Back in their apartment, Michael ordered Jan to pack a suitcase with her new clothes, and by noon they were on a bus to Portland, just across the state line into Oregon.

During the winter months of early 1977 Jan and Michael lived in a seedy hotel near the river in downtown Portland. Then they moved out to Spokane, and for a while Jan enjoyed hanging out in the twilight zone of derelicts and hookers. They made friends in their new hotel and settled into the role of fugitives. Soon, however, Jan noticed that Michael's behavior was becoming more and more macho, especially when male friends came to hang out in their room. As spring came on, Jan began to chafe under his domineering personality. On the morning of the last day of May the two had a scene. Michael accused her of being lazy and not keeping their room neat and clean. Jan fumed. Then, to impress one of his friends with his control over his woman, Michael ordered her to tidy up, and to punctuate his message, he swatted Jan with a kitchen towel as he and his buddy went out the door, slamming it behind him.

Jan flew into a rage. Like a whirlwind she destroyed any semblance of order in the room, screaming like a banshee all the while. Finally, when she came to her senses, a plan had formed in her mind. She would escape. The most important man in her life, John Lash, was now living in Hollywood. She would seek refuge with him for a while, get on her feet, and start over again. Jan grew calm and proceeded to pack the bare essentials for her getaway in a single suitcase. When she was ready, she sneaked down the hotel service elevator and out the back door. At the Greyhound station, she discovered that she was just in time for a southbound bus. She felt somehow invulnerable, and she took it as a beneficent omen when the ticket clerk told her that today was the last day for special cheap rates. As the bus rolled out past the edge of town and through the arid valleys south of Spokane, Jan contemplated her own "weakness for assholes," and heaved a big sigh of relief.

When she arrived in LA Jan discovered that John was having an affair with the wife of a local TV news anchor, and for a while she enjoyed the peace and quiet of hanging out alone in his apartment. She explored the sprawling city for the first time, and even located the little house in which her mother had spent her girlhood during the Depression. Eventually, she tired of her idleness and found a job at Mark Hines Creations, a pottery manufacturer, where she made faces for the decorative pots and had a brief affair with the owner, who took her on her first trip to Hawaii.

Then another strange coincidence occurred. One day Jan spotted a notice for extras for the first Orion Pictures film, which turned out to be an adaptation of Carolyn Cassady's *Heart Beat*, a memoir of her life with Neal, the model for Dean Moriarty, the protagonist of *On the Road*, and her love affair with Jack Kerouac in the early 1950s. Nick Nolte was playing Neal, Sissy Spacek was cast as Carolyn herself, and John Heard would act the role of Jack Kerouac. Jan recognized serendipity when she saw it, and she left work to try out for a bit part in a movie about her own father.

Naturally, the moviemakers were thrilled when she turned up on the set, as were the actors, especially Nolte, who credited his reading of Kerouac's novel with inspiring him to leave home and follow a career in acting. When Carolyn first caught sight of Jan, she exclaimed, "It's just like seeing a ghost!" Then, regaining her composure, she invited Jan to visit her in Los Gatos, and perhaps Jan got some insight into her own reasons for writing from Carolyn's success. In the end, ironically, Jan's scene was cut from *Heart Beat*. Even her attempt at imaginary participation in her father's life was thwarted. Still, working as an extra made her life in LA more exciting, and during the remainder of her sixteen months there, she continued to find small parts in other movies, developing in the process quite a taste for performance.

NINE

JAN KEROUAC THE NOVELIST

Jan's homecoming at her mother's new place at 605 1/2 Ruby Street, just north of downtown Ellensburg, signaled the beginning of a new era for her, if not for Joan. Her brother, David, took her dumpster-diving at the Albertson's supermarket just up the street, and together they discovered they could make butter out of discarded whipping cream. They froze pound after pound of it to use for holiday baking. But when she got settled, Jan took an unexpected step: she enrolled for classes at Central Washington University during the spring quarter of 1979. Her placement scores put her in an upper-level Spanish class, and even though she was by this time almost ten years older than most of the kids on campus, she enjoyed her professors' praise, and for a while it looked like she might make a serious student. But again fate intervened, this time in the form of the latest Kerouac biographer, Gerald Nicosia.

In his relentless pursuit of everyone who knew Jack Kerouac, Gerry had tracked Joan down to her small cabin in Kittitas and come to interview her on tape. Naturally, he became interested in Jan as well, and he suggested that she try to publish an excerpt of her novel-in-progress in Lawrence Ferlinghetti's *City Lights Journal*. Sure enough, Ferlinghetti accepted a version of chapter 12, which describes the beginning of her journey through Central and South America. Gerry also invited her to appear with him at a National Society of Arts and Letters award banquet in Chicago, and in October 1979 he arranged for her to come down to San Francisco to participate in a reading at the Spaghetti Factory to commemorate the tenth anniversary of her father's death. By this time Jan had a finished draft of *Baby Driver*, which she was still calling *Everthreads*, and while she was in the Bay Area, Gerry introduced her to a literary agent, Joyce Cole. This led ultimately to a contract with St. Martin's Press, and suddenly, after a decade of wandering and writing, Jan became a published novelist. Her editor, Barbara Anderson, suggested the book might be more interesting if they altered the straightforward chronological narrative by alternating chapters from different periods of Jan's life. She also proposed a new title. So *Baby Driver*, as it now stands, begins in the late 1960s, then reaches back to Jan's childhood, creating by this scheme an effective contrast between her adult life and her early years.

The unexpected result of St. Martin's acceptance of her novel was a $10,000 advance on royalties. In her new frame of mind, Jan decided to clear up some legal issues that were still haunting her, namely a warrant for her arrest on a charge of fraud outstanding in the state of Washington. With the help of her new boyfriend, Scott Robinson, Jan hired an Ellensburg lawyer, Kenneth Beckley Jr., to handle her case. In the summer and fall, as the ash from nearby Mount Saint Helens drifted down on the Kittitas Valley like strange grey summer snow, the attorney worked to get the charge against Jan reduced to a misdemeanor. When she finally appeared in circuit court to plead guilty, Jan was surprised when the local judge sentenced her to only five days in jail. She found she could even serve her time on weekends, if she wanted. At first, she determined to do the whole five days at the same time to get it over with, but once in her cell, her mind filled with memories of the girls' reformatory in the Bronx, and she arranged with Bruce, the jailer, who happened to be Scott's father, to let her out. After a week's worth of decent food and several long baths, she would feel strong enough to finish her sentence.

Jan had met Scott at a New Year's Eve party at the home of her old pal, Malcolm Connover, Bernard's former roommate. During Jan's absence Malcolm had hooked up with a single mother, a woman named Caroline, who was also a friend of Joan's. Bernard was visiting from New York, where he had been working as a janitor in a whorehouse. Predictably, he was full of crazy stories about his job. Jan hadn't seen him since she shut the door on him at her apartment in Tacoma, and she thought he looked bigger and healthier. Malcolm and Caroline introduced her to a rather prissy young man, and Jan — somewhat to her surprise — felt attracted to him. A couple months later, in the dead of Washington winter, she ran into him outside the Liberty Theatre, a landmark in Ellensburg with its tall 1940s marquee. Scott, who rented a loft above the theater, invited her up for "a cup of tea and a bubblebath." Jan perceived immediately that he was inexperienced with women, and she proceeded to deflower him that same night.

Though their relationship was always strained and contentious because of Scott's overrefined taste, he and Jan stayed together for over two years, through four different apartments. *People* magazine sent a reporter and photographer to Ellensburg to do a story on the famous novelist's literary daughter. For this piece, which ran in the "Heirs" section of the magazine during Christmas week of 1981, the reporter, Jim Calio, asked Jan to pose in the bathtub, while Scott incongruously took her blood pressure. Meanwhile, the photographer somehow squirmed through the small bathroom window overhead. The bizarre result is a bird's-eye view of Jan peeking up through her bubblebath while Scott looks intently down at the gauge on the sphygmomanometer. Thus began Jan's career as a celebrity.

In April 1981 Jan found an excuse to end her unsatisfying relationship with Scott and get back on the road. The previous year her mother had moved down to Eugene, Oregon, to be near her other daughters. Kathy, who had gone to high school in Ellensburg, subsequently enrolled at the University of Oregon, and Sharon had stayed in Eugene after graduating from high school there. In half a day Jan had relocated, joining her mother and David in a small house on Bell Avenue in the Bethel Triangle neighborhood of west Eugene. Joan had become a neighborhood activist, fighting to create a park in her neighborhood, which was sandwiched in between two sets of railroad tracks. From this location Jan got the idea for her second novel, which she would call *Trainsong*. Soon she found a job baking bread for one of Eugene's better restaurants, the Excelsior Cafe.

Thanks to the publication of *Baby Driver* and the public relations efforts of Gerry Nicosia, Jan's whereabouts became known to

Kerouac fans. Early in 1982 Jan began to receive letters embossed with a large red dharma wheel, invitations from the Naropa Institute to attend a celebration of the twenty-fifth anniversary of the publication of *On the Road* to be held that coming summer in Boulder. With characteristic nonchalance, Jan disregarded them until one afternoon a busboy at the restaurant came into the kitchen looking unusually excited.

"What is it?" Jan inquired of the young man.

"It's Ken Kesey," he stammered. "He's outside and he wants to talk to you."

Kesey, the well-known novelist, psychedelic theater crusader, and local character, had tracked Jan down to see if she wanted to ride east with him to the Naropa celebration. Jan was flattered and impressed. She had never had trouble finding excitement, but now it looked as though the fun and games were escalating to a higher level. She was getting a reputation. Though the drive with Kesey, which would have made a fascinating story in itself, never materialized, he did convince Jan to go to Boulder for the conference, and though they flew out on separate flights, they ended up staying next door to each other for ten days once they arrived.

Jan took to Boulder's hip atmosphere immediately, and though she didn't have much use for her father's fans and admirers, she made herself available at the conference, where she found opportunity to renew her acquaintance with her former Lower East Side neighbors Allen Ginsberg and Peter Orlovsky, see Carolyn Cassady again, and meet Jack's first wife, Edie Parker. Sampas connections were conspicuously absent at the Boulder affair, but contact with them lay only months in the future. At a soiree in the elegant old Boulderado Hotel, Jan fell into conversation with John Steinbeck Jr., then into his lap, and finally into bed with the other famous literary heir. What offspring might have come from that match!

Alas, the attraction was short-lived, but Jan gained a revolutionary insight into her own situation from Steinbeck: she learned she was entitled to royalties from her father's works. Since the copyright law at that time still specified that the first renewal came twenty-seven years after publication, and they were in Boulder to celebrate the twenty-fifth anniversary of the publication of *On the Road*, Jan would soon be eligible to add her name to that of Stella Sampas on the copyright page of her father's most famous novel. Among other things, Steinbeck put her in touch with the scion of another American literary family, Aram Saroyan. Suddenly, after a mere ten days, Jan felt as though she had found her niche. After taping some video sessions that eventually became part of the film *What Happened to Kerouac?*, Jan flew back to Eugene, announced her new plan to Joan and David, packed up her belongings into just nine boxes, and returned to Boulder to establish her residence there.

At Naropa, the nation's first and only Buddhist college, Jan had also taken an interest in the Tibetan Buddhism practiced there by Naropa's founder, Chogyam Trungpa. She had a standing invitation from Allen and Peter to crash with them at their house on Bluff Street, which she now took them up on. Within a couple months, however, she found her own room in a house across the street from the one supposedly occupied by Mork and Mindy in the popular TV show of the day. One of her housemates was, as Jan recalled in *Trainsong*, "a well-hung Buddhist plumber" she called Malcolm. They hit it off during a massage Malcolm offered as a housewarming gift, and straightaway he dumped his girlfriend and attached himself to Jan. The two stayed together rather happily until Jan's wanderlust got the better of her. Meanwhile, in view of her coming acquisition of royalties, Jan thought to make her break from Bernard official, and on July 18, 1983, the Boulder County district court referee dissolved their eight-year marriage.

Her next opportunity to travel was provided gratis by her German publisher. *Baby Driver* had been translated (by an Italian couple, ironically) and become a cult hit in Europe. In October 1983 she flew to Amsterdam, the first stop on her reading tour. She opened her set at the famous literary coffeehouse, Melkveg, with an elegy for her stillborn child, Natasha, which she had never read before. It cast an eerie spell over both the audience and herself. The crowd lionized her, in spite of the presence of several other counterculture writers, including the ill-fated Richard Brautigan, the head of the hippie novelists. In the early 1960s a young Dutch writer had created a Beat scene in Holland with the publication of his autobiographical fiction *I, Jan Cremer*, and the trend had spread into Germany, where weirdness takes the weirdest shapes, and continued into the 1980s. Jan always found her admirers lined up and waiting to talk after her performances. In Amsterdam she also renewed her brief acquaintance with William S. Burroughs, her father's best friend and strongest philosophical influence, who was now on tour himself with his secretary, James Grauerholz.

From Amsterdam Jan proceeded to Paris, arriving in the City of Light on the fourteenth anniversary of her father's death, October 21, 1983. After some difficulty locating her French publisher's office, Jan checked into a hotel, where she made friends with a Latin American desk clerk, and proceeded to take herself shopping on the rue Jacob. She told me in 1995 that during this stay she also had a brief affair with Grauerholz, who had followed her to Paris with Burroughs. The bulk of Jan's tour, a series of dates in various German cities, remained, so she hastened toward Berlin, met on the way by a German television producer named Martin, who was to act as her guide. Predictably, the two also became lovers, and Martin squired her past Checkpoint Charlie into the still divided city. On All Saints' Day he took her for a visit to East Berlin, and the high point of her second trip to Europe came when Communist police threatened to detain Martin because of his haircut and the way he was dressed. Jan fled from the gloomy land back into the West, and she was home in Boulder for the new year, 1984.

Trainsong ends with an account of Jan's extended vacation to Baja California with Malcolm. After dropping acid on sunny tropical beaches for a couple months, Malcolm needed to return to the leaky faucets and clogged toilets of Boulder, and Jan decided to take this opportunity to part ways with him. She went north, but only as far as Santa Fe, where she rejoined her first husband, John Lash, who had returned to the Southwest to make it his new base of operations. His girlfriend, Lucy Cornwall, introduced Jan to a local lawyer, Saul Cohen, who began the legal work necessary for Jan to begin receiving royalties from her father's work. Negotiating with Sterling Lord, who had been Jack

Kerouac's agent, Cohen arranged for the revision of the copyright of *On the Road* as it was in the process of being renewed. Apparently, no one at that time questioned Jan's paternity, and henceforth, she began to share the royalties with Stella Sampas. Well over a million copies of the novel were in print, and in the next few years many of Jack's other novels would come up for copyright renewal.

One day while Jan was still in Santa Fe, getting reacquainted with her old haunts, the first check came from the Lord Agency in care of John. Jan opened it, glanced at the amount, disappointed that it was only $700. She handed the check to John, who looked at it more carefully. "Look again," he said, handing it back to her. The check was for $7,000. Jan took John by the arm and led him down to her favorite nightclub on Canyon Road, El Farol, where she announced to the bartender in classic fashion, "Drinks for everyone."

Seven thousand dollars may not seem like a lot of money, but to a young woman used to partying on a lot less, it represented yet another step toward the jet set. Jan had no concept of saving, since she had never had much to begin with, and since she had usually been paid in the form of paychecks, she neglected to notice that federal income tax had not been deducted from her royalty check. Oblivious to the dangers of her new prosperity, she started to plan a third trip to Europe, on the pretext of visiting her sister Kathy, who had married a Greek Cypriot and settled with him on the divided island. Jan's trip led her beyond Nicosia, however, and she wound up living in a wacky pension on the Greek mainland for several months. The people she met there provided her with more characters for a new novel, though she did not realize it until the following year. The household revolved around a German/Greek mother who doted on her two children. Jan became involved with the son, Nikos, who tried to kill himself by running his car exhaust into the back window of the car while it was idling. Though he was unsuccessful in his suicide attempt, everyone in the household was understandably upset, including Jan. Nevertheless, she respected Nikos' mystical temperament, and she recalled vividly an occurrence that happened during one of their walks in the country. Jan and he were discussing the differences between America and Greece, using a potpourri of terms from various languages. Frustrated by his inability to express himself clearly, Nikos dug his foot in the earth. "This," he hissed, "is Greece." According to Jan, a little trickle of water sprang out of his footstep, and pretty soon a little spring had begun to flow from the spot, just as in the lives of the saints.

Back in the States, things were more mundane, but the checks from Sterling Lord kept coming, though somewhat erratically, Jan thought. Interest in her father had heated up, and the manuscript of her second novel was being considered for publication by Henry Holt. Jan was invited to attend a conference honoring her father's Canadian roots in Quebec in October 1987, and she eagerly accepted, looking forward to meeting some of her distant cousins, perhaps, and to learning a bit of the local French dialect. In Quebec City, avoiding as usual the fans and admirers of her dad, Jan fell in with several members of the Deschamps family, and although she was attracted to the older brother, she had a fling with François instead. She felt that the whole family was coming on to her, however, even the boys' sister. She went back home to Montreal with François, and after a stroll out on the ice on the frozen St. Lawrence River one night, she astounded both herself and her lover by inserting his ATM card into a machine and guessing his PIN correctly. The money they spent in the bars on the rue Ste. Catherine that night seemed magical.

Earlier in the year, in the spring of 1987, Jan had had another encounter with ice, this time at a conference at John Lash's alma mater, the University of Maine at Orono. Fleeing from those she had dubbed the Academia Nuts, Jan and her new local beau decided to take an early spring canoe ride on the flooded Penobscot River. Not only were they swept off by the rapid current, but soon they noticed that the water was filled with chunks of ice that came scraping against the hull of their boat. Somehow by paddling furiously the two made it back to land, and Jan rewarded her boyfriend for the excitement with a tryst in her hotel room.

After the conference she headed down to New York City, where she had agreed to apartment-sit for some friends who had gone off to Europe for an extended holiday. One of her main duties was to take care of the friends' parrot, and one day as she was walking down 5th Avenue, her recent experiences began to take the shape of a novel. Because of her pet-sitting chores, she decided to call the new book *Parrot Fever*. A few moments later she passed a newsstand, where the headlines of the New York papers blared out the news of the Chernobyl disaster. Recalling her brush with death on the Penobscot, Jan combined the two events into a title for her first chapter: "Chernobyl Swan." Filled with her own imaginative glee, she popped into the next coffee shop she passed, hailed the waiter, and ordered coffee and a cesium danish. She got coffee and a cheese pastry, and the waiter's diffidence lightened her mood further.

In LA after her visit to Canada, Jan got news that Holt had accepted her second novel, *Trainsong*. She used the advance to pay off her bills, and on a dare from her friends, she bought a plane ticket for Hawaii. After she paid for the ticket, she had only about $400 left in her pocket. She decided that would have to do, and without hesitating, took off into the Pacific.

No stranger to living by her wits, Jan talked her way into a duplex in a run-down section of Maui without a deposit and set about finding a job. By this time she had amassed a good deal of kitchen experience and was capable of working as a gourmet cook. Within days, in January 1988, she landed a job in a restaurant/condo complex by the ocean. Soon she got involved with a co-worker at the restaurant, a fellow named Michael Lynch, "a dark character," she called him, who was fond of mixing Xanax, Valium, and alcohol. "I called it a 'disastrophe,'" Jan told me in 1995, "and I feel like I'm still in it."

Michael neglected to tell Jan was that he was married, and one day his wife discovered them together in Michael's house and left in a predictable huff. It so happened that Michael had recently stolen a huge hunk of fish from the restaurant and was thawing it to fix for dinner. While he and Jan were waiting for the fish to thaw, they decided to go to a nearby Foodland to pick up a bottle of Jack Daniel's. "We were taken over by a demon — you can almost see its picture on the label on the bottle," Jan said. To add to the chaos, Michael's dog, Shane, was missing, so he kept going to the back door of his shack in this trashy area of Maui and yelling for the dog. Pretty soon, he and Jan got into a little game of saying, "You'd better not have any more of that whiskey," and snatching the bottle away from each other to take a swig. Before they knew it, the bottle was empty. Then, out of nowhere, Michael produced a baseball bat, and enraged by Shane's departure (Jan said the dog probably sensed the evil vibrations and split), he started smashing out the glass in the huge patio doors. Through her alcohol haze Jan realized, "Oh oh, he's lost it," but when she tried to approach him in her bare feet, Michael grabbed her out of concern that she would cut herself, carried her to the bedroom door, and threw her forcefully on the bed. Then he went back to smashing glass.

Collecting her wits, Jan decided it was time to make her escape. She opened the bedroom window and put one leg through to crawl out, but she lost her balance and fell on the ground, putting a nasty gash in the top of her head in the process. She was so drunk, however, that she failed to notice the flow of blood. Then she took off down the street, barefoot, trying to reach the home of some people she knew in the neighborhood. When she reached their house, she ran into a tent they had pitched in the backyard and huddled there in fear. The neighbors, for their part, seeing the blood matting her hair and fearing that she had been attacked, called the police.

From her hiding place Jan heard the sound of sirens approaching and crept out, intending to return to Michael's house to warn him. But when she saw the cops arriving, she fled. Nearing a ditch filled with weeds, she said to herself, "Centipedes, here I come," and dived into the undergrowth. After the police had handcuffed Michael and put him in the wagon, they spotted Jan and took her down to the station for interrogation. Even though it turned out that no one had committed any crime, Michael's wife used the incident to obtain a restraining order forbidding Michael and Jan to have any contact with each other. Sometime later, when she decided to include this episode in *Parrot Fever*, Jan thought to title the chapter "Fired from Paradise."

In the midst of Jan's six-month drug orgy, the advance copies of *Trainsong* arrived, but she had practically forgotten that she was a published author. Years later she recalled looking at the book and thinking, "Wow, I wrote a book." Just holding a copy of her second novel in her hand, she said, restored her self-esteem. The publisher, Holt, had arranged a U.S. book tour for her, but she spent the travel allowance on drugs. When that was gone, she called New York and asked for more money. When that came, she spent it on more drugs. "Paradise had turned into purgatory," she later observed.

She had several other experiences in Hawaii, including a chance meeting with Steely Dan's Walter Becker on the beach. Michael also enticed her into participating in an acid trip, during which he stole his wife's jeep and bounced it off several rental cars full of horrified tourists on the way to a secluded beach, where he and Jan hallucinated communing with a baby whale. This time, despite her altered state of mind, Jan eluded the police when they arrived. Finally, somehow, she was able to extricate herself at the last moment and go on the book tour.

The publicity surrounding the release of *Trainsong* brought Jan another conference invitation, but this time it was something out of the ordinary. Jack's supporters in Lowell had been lobbying the city council for years for some public recognition of their favorite son. Finally, the money had been approved, a site set aside, and an artist commissioned to create a Kerouac memorial in Jack's hometown. Jan was one of the few women officially invited to the dedication of the memorial that spring. Even the founder of Kerouac studies, Ann Charters, had been excluded, presumably on account of Stella Sampas's distaste for her biography. In fact, John Sampas told me in 1996 that a bodyguard had been hired for the event to keep all Kerouac's biographers — especially Gerry Nicosia — away from Stella. Charters came on her own, as did several other women who had been associated with Kerouac, including Joyce Johnson, who later published her outsider's account of the festivities in *Vanity Fair*. Johnson attempted to befriend Jan, who felt awkward in the presence of all the "ghouls," as she thought of her father's fans. Later Johnson mailed Jan a drawing done by Jack Kerouac that had come into Joyce's possession. It was the only thing of her father's that Jan ever owned. But Jan was standoffish with Johnson, and downright offended by Ann Charters.

Jan Kerouac publicity photo, 1994

A young Kerouac aficionado from Berkeley named Stephen Ronan had more success befriending the great man's daughter. Stephen wrote of his encounter with Jan in a lively little self-published book called *Lowell Journal 1988*. In it he included a telling photograph of Jan, who at some point in their wanderings in Lowell had suspended herself over an open trash can. After he went home to California, Jan sent him a couple postcards recalling their time together fondly.

For her part, Jan felt that other people in Lowell were staring at her, especially at Edson Cemetery, where she visited her father's grave for the first time. "Oh look," she imagined the voyeurs saying as they snapped her picture, "there's Jack's daughter crying at his grave." In later years she frequently referred to Lowell as the Twilight Zone.

After the dedication of the Kerouac memorial in Lowell, Jan tarried briefly in New York City, then went back to the West Coast to be near her mother, who was dying of breast cancer. The disease had been in remission since a year or two after she was first diagnosed in the early 1980s, but lately Jan's mother had taken a turn for the worse. The ravages of cancer had made Joan sensitive about her appearance, and Jan found when she got to Eugene that her mother refused help from the family, preferring to let a woman she hired to clean her house run personal errands and look after her private needs. Jan felt somewhat helpless, but she could see by the look of things that she had better settle down in Oregon for a while.

In the past three years Jan had already learned to count on the checks from the Lord Agency, and even though the checks began to come in larger and larger amounts as a Kerouac revival gathered steam, she managed to spend whatever she got. One way she disposed of her money in Eugene was to loan $8,000 to her new boyfriend, who wanted to start a cab company. Perhaps more sensible of the risk than Jan, he named it Odyssey Taxi. Carter Webb Neely was a Chicagoan, and his city ways charmed Jan, even though she quickly realized he was two-timing her. The reason she didn't care was that for the first time in her life — she was now thirty-six — she began to feel actual sexual passion for a man. She thought of it as the fulfillment of all her sensual escapades, and for the time being, she could care less whether he paid back her loan or stayed faithful to her. For the first time in her life, she was just enjoying balling a guy. When Jan became pregnant during their relationship Carter claimed, "It couldn't be me. I been shooting blanks all along." He explained this by telling Jan that he had been hit in the nuts with a crab apple when he was a boy. Jan admitted that there was a "very small possibility" that the child was someone else's. It was her eighth and last pregnancy. When she had an abortion, she didn't tell her mother, the first time in her life she had ever withheld anything from her.

In the summer of 1989 Joan's family gathered in Eugene to bid her farewell. Her brother Dave flew up from Atlanta. It was the first time he had seen his only sister since she moved briefly to Seattle in 1969 before settling in Kittitas. Kathy came all the way from Cyprus, even though she and Joan fought as they always had, reminding Jan that Kathy was "the least favorite daughter." Joan was an excellent storyteller, though she tended to embellish and even invent material if she felt the urge. Prompted by Dave's presence, she told her children stories they had heard a million times, as well as stories they had never heard before at all. Her stable, conservative brother caught up with all the doings of his nieces and nephew, as well as with the events of his sister's life during the past twenty years. She looked feeble, and Dave sensed that they had better enjoy themselves this summer, because they might not have another chance.

As it turned out, he was right. Joan succumbed to the disease on Mother's Day 1990. For some reason, neither Jan nor her brother David expected their mother to die in the hospital, and they were actually discussing whether to move her to a nursing home when she died. Jan recalled sitting at home that Sunday, depressed about Carter, when the phone rang. When she described this to me in 1995, Jan imitated the nurse's reedy voice, which failed to simulate a tone of concern: "Miss Kerouac, your mother has died." At first Jan felt nothing, just as when she had learned of her father's death over twenty years before. Rather, thoughts of the nurse she had just spoken to filled her head. "Why is she using that tone of voice?" Jan wondered. "She must have a whole list of people to call and she's trying to sound concerned. That's it, she's trying to sound concerned." But the nurse's professional manner only served to numb the pain temporarily. Later it began to hit Jan that her mother was gone for good.

Despite her growing income, neither Jan nor her brother and sisters had enough money to pay for the funeral, so they made the arrangements with the undertaker, and when their Uncle Dave arrived from Atlanta, he took care of the $1,100 bill. "It was really a pauper's funeral," Jan said, and because her mother had been in failing health for so long, the casket was closed for the service. "My mother already looked dead when she died," Jan recalled. She had never been in a funeral home before, and was surprised by how normal it seemed. She was also surprised by the large number of mourners who appeared to pay their respects to her mother. She and her brother had brought some of Joan's personal possessions to the visitation, and soon they found themselves giggling at their own grisly jokes. "My mother often laughed at her own death in those last years," Jan said, "and so David and I thought our black humor was right in her spirit." Joan's body was cremated and her ashes still rest in an urn on the mantel in her daughter Sharon's home in Eugene.

That fall, Carter talked Jan into dancing in two Eugene strip bars, Jiggles and the Great Alaskan Bush Company. He merely wanted to brag to his buddies and his other girlfriend that he was dating a stripper, but Jan, who loved to dance under any circumstances, derived some satisfaction from her exhibitionism. Late in December 1990, however, just seven months after her mother's death, Jan left Eugene to spend Christmas with her old friends in Ellensburg. She planned to be home in her apartment in Eugene the day before New Year's Eve, but she was delayed for eleven hours in the Portland bus station. The depot was jammed with stranded travelers, and not a seat was empty.

As Jan tried to while away the hours of waiting, severe cramps hit her. By now she thought she knew the symptoms, but no bleeding followed. She managed to hold on through the short bus trip back to Eugene, but when she arrived she was in so much pain that she called a cab — not Odyssey — to take her to her apartment. The night was very cold, especially for Oregon, and

Jan climbed the frosted outdoor stairs to her apartment with difficulty. By now it was late on New Year's Eve. When Jan reached her own front door, she took out her keys. Dismayed, she realized that Carter had inadvertently substituted another set of keys for her own before she left town and that she was locked out of her own home. It came to her that the only way she could get in was to break a window, something she had never done before. Nevertheless, she used her boot to smash the large plate-glass front window, then picked out the jagged pieces so she could climb in safely. "I didn't want to drag my crotch across a jagged piece of glass at that point," she said with grim humor.

Shut up in her bedroom to keep out the cold air blowing in through the broken window, she tried to rest and relax, but the pain grew worse. Finally, she called an ambulance, which took her to the hospital. She recalls that the doctor who attended her had been taking the decorations off his Christmas tree when the hospital paged him. Unable to determine the extent of Jan's illness even after performing a laparotomy, he recommended an exploratory operation. Jan consented, and seven hours later, on New Year's Day 1991, she awoke with "the worst hangover in the world, but not from drinking." She said she felt "like a ninety-nine-year-old woman."

What the doctor had discovered after he opened Jan up "with an incision very much like a cesarean incision" was that her fallopian tubes had become fused to her bowel walls by a previous infection. The compassionate doctor spent his New Year's Eve carefully separating Jan's tubes from the surrounding tissue. While Jan was recuperating at home a week later, the itemized hospital bills began to pour in. With no money, and feeling guilty about not being able to repay the kindness of her doctor, Jan laid plans to fake her own death in Puerto Rico. That seemed the appropriate place to work her plan, since she had first met Carter on her way to Cuba and had canceled that trip to pursue the ill-fated romance. Her friends warned her not to travel, especially to a warm place where she would be tempted to swim. When she left Oregon, the scar from her operation had still not quite healed. "Just like magic," Jan claimed years later, "my scar healed by the time I arrived in Puerto Rico." She began to feel remarkably well, considering the nightmare she had just endured.

When she first arrived in Puerto Rico, Jan had problems convinc-ing the hotel where she was staying that she was not a prostitute, but soon she was rescued by a handsome young Puerto Rican man named Jose Antonio Robles, who took her to live with him in his apartment in the small town of Carolina, in the northeast corner of the island, where Jan settled down to recuperate from her operation. She forgot about her plan to fake her own death. The couple got on fairly well, but when Jose started to verbally abuse her, Jan began to look for a way out. Once again, her blue-water paradise had turned to purgatory. In February 1991 she found an opportunity to escape when James Austin of Rhino Records invited Jan to accompany him to the Grammy Awards. Austin had high hopes that the recently released box set of Jack Kerouac recordings would win in the spoken-word category, and he wanted Jack's daughter, who had granted her permission for the recordings and even written a blurb for the liner notes, to be there to share the expected honor with him and his company. Her brother David also wrote to inform his sister that he was getting married in Missoula, Montana. Jan could piggyback on the Rhino trip to attend the wedding.

Whether it was the belated effects of her operation, from which she had probably not recovered sufficiently, or the partying at the Grammies and at David's hippie wedding, by the time she returned to Puerto Rico in March, Jan knew she was ailing. Still, she figured that rest and relaxation would soon put her back on her feet. Jose was glad to have her back, and her absence had soothed their relations, so she settled down to the task of doing as little as possible. She basked in the sun and swam in the ocean. Her skin grew brown in the tropical climate. She felt comfortable, but for some reason her strength did not return as quickly as she expected it to. By May she was beginning to wonder if she shouldn't see a doctor, and then one day in early June, she collapsed.

When she awoke in a San Juan hospital, she discovered a nasty wound in the crook of her left elbow. When she looked up, she saw IV bottles hanging on a rack behind her head. Slowly, her bewildered senses put it all together, and she realized where she was. When the charge nurse found that Jan was conscious, she sent for the doctors, who informed Jan that she had suffered total kidney failure. The missing vein in her forearm had been implanted in her belly to serve as a peritoneal catheter. Without a transplant, she would be forced to undergo regular daily dialysis for the rest of her life, and they gave her only ten years to live, at the outside. Jan Kerouac was thirty-nine years old.

TEN

NOBODY'S WIFE

In the spring of 1964 Stella Sampas got a phone call. She vaguely recognized the drunken voice, but when the caller announced that his name was Jack Kerouac, Stella was skeptical. She suspected a trick, so she asked one of her brothers to investigate. When he came back to the house, he did indeed have Jack Kerouac in tow. But Jack was drunk, terribly drunk. He was contemplating moving back from Florida to Hyannis on Cape Cod, hoping to enjoy the Atlantic gloom without being bothered by groupies or tempted to spend his nights in the bars of Lowell. He had also become obsessed with his heritage, and he wanted to be close enough to Boston to use the Harvard libraries for his genealogical research. Yet this night he seemed to be on a mission. Stella asked him why he had come. "I've come to marry you," was his simple reply.

And marry her he did, in November 1966, only a month after his mother had suffered a severe stroke that left her partially paralyzed. The civil ceremony was held at Jack and Gabrielle's house in Hyannis, rather than in the bride's home, and soon after they were married Jack and Stella decided to move back to Lowell for the sake of convenience. Because of the move and since Jack and his mother already operated a household, Stella never unwrapped most of the presents she got at the wedding shower her sister threw for her in Lowell. Three decades later many of these same gifts, still unopened, remain in the home Jack and Stella shared in Florida, which is now owned by her family. In 1967 Jack tried to buy one of his childhood homes, but they ended up in a new split-level in the same section of town as the Sampas family.

Jack quickly established his routine: a bit of writing during the day, massive drinking and carousing at night, and hours of long-

Jack and Stella in a family snapshot, 1966

distance phone calls to old friends — including his first wife, Edie Parker — in the wee hours. Never one to live beyond her means, Stella begged Jack to control his behavior to keep from destroying himself and ruining the family financially. At the same time, she was forced both to care for Gabrielle, who was not exactly a teetotaler, and to accept her criticism of Stella's housekeeping. I imagine this criticism involved a good bit of ethnic prejudice on Gabrielle's part, mixed with a measure of jealousy that her role of caregiver to her son had been taken over by another younger, yet capable and motherly woman.

As Jack's drinking grew worse, his nightly exploits became the subject of mirth in a gossip column written by one of the Sampas in-laws for the local newspaper. Stella tried everything in her power to keep the man she loved from humiliating himself. She asked him to stay home in the evenings and hid his clothes for insurance. He went out in his bathrobe and got arrested for public indecency. She nagged him to hang up when he stayed on the phone too long. He merely shouted curses at her. Their phone bills became astronomical. And fortunately, Lowell was still a small town, and Jack had made drinking buddies out of most of the cops on the night beat. Still, when he grew too abusive and crude, they threw him in the drunk tank, and his bail and fines were so much more money down the drain. To put things in perspective, I suspect that this outrageous behavior was simply a feature of milltown life in Stella's view. After all, one of her brothers, Nicky, owned one of the bars Jack frequented. Alcoholism, unlike madness, is a pattern of behavior most Americans adapt to rather than reject, especially when the drunkard is a member of their family. Stella wasn't born yesterday. She saw Jack's weakness as another cross for her to bear, but she was strong, and he was her husband, so she carried on bravely.

The same way with her mother-in-law. Gabrielle was certainly not the first demanding invalid that Stella had ever waited on. Her whole life was a pattern of caregiving. She hardly knew how to be selfish. And for Stella, in-laws were members of one's family. She did get a measure of relief when Gabrielle agreed to go down to Boston for inpatient physical therapy, but after a few weeks the old lady asked to be brought home, claiming that being around other invalids all day long made her depressed, as I'm sure it did. Some outsiders who observed her at this time perceived that she had recovered full physical function, and some suspected that she kept up a front of disability to exercise her hold on her son, but others recall the paralysis of her left side as permanent. Whatever the case, Stella was in it for the duration. She had married the man she had loved since girlhood, and marriage was for life in her book.

The damp cold of the New England winter began to bother Gabrielle, who had grown accustomed to Florida in her middle age. She fussed and complained mightily, but neither Jack nor Stella had any desire to move out of Lowell, and despite Jack's behavior, Stella at least had the help and sympathy of friends and relatives, while in Florida she would be all on her own in a strange place. Except for vacations, Stella had never been out of Lowell. But Gabrielle's demands grew stronger, rather than weaker, as the winter wore on. Before they moved, however, Stella suffered two very different shocks.

First, she and Jack had sex for the first time. She bled so profusely that she had to be taken to the hospital. Nicosia describes the event as a marital rape, but John Sampas rejects that version of the events. Nicosia also records that with almost unbelievable callousness Kerouac later invited some of his male buddies into the house to show them the bloodstains on the carpet. Taking them upstairs, he proceeded to drop his trousers and, referring to the small size of his penis, marvel out loud that he had been able to accomplish such a prodigious feat with such a puny instrument. What Stella's reaction was we will probably never know, because, as I say, she was raised in a Victorian household where sex was never mentioned. Aside from the public embarrassment of having to visit a small-town hospital after such a private incident, however, I think it is safe to assume that her attitude toward the man she had "saved herself for" — if toward sex in general — might not have been the same after that night.

The second event came in the fall of 1967. By this time Stella had learned to fend off itinerant hippies who came on a pilgrimage to visit the King of the Beats, so she was prepared when a familiar-looking fifteen-year-old girl showed up at the door seeking an interview. This one came with unusual credentials, however. She had stopped first with her older boyfriend at the home of one of Jack's cousins, Herve, whose name she had found in the Lowell phonebook. Herve's wife, Doris, immediately perceived the family likeness, although she didn't know that Jack had a daughter. Yet here she was, a dead ringer for her old man. Doris sent for Tony Sampas, Stella's brother, who drove Jan right over to her dad's house on Sanders Avenue in the Highlands. Whether Stella recognized the resemblance has not been recorded. Needless to say, she viewed herself by this time mainly as protector of her home. If that required turning away well-meaning people who might tempt Jack to go on another binge, so be it. Earlier in the fall Jack had had to resort to subterfuge to accommodate three young writers who had come up from New York City to interview him for *The Paris Review*. Stella therefore admitted the girl cautiously, and she may have noticed that Jan was pregnant. Her companion, a young man with hair much too long, lagged behind.

The house was empty of the Greek and French relatives who frequently visited. As usual, Jack was drinking heavily and watching TV. Pop culture critics of today might find in his choice of shows an act of wish-fulfillment: he was watching *The Beverly Hillbillies*, that wacky — but essentially happy — lower-class family that had struck it rich and determined to make Hollywood conform to its values, rather than the other way around. Stella took in the scene of Jan taking in the scene, though Jan seems not to have paid any attention to her stepmother. Naturally, her eyes were focused on her father's eyes. Stella also noticed when Jan made a touching gesture, though it was hard for her to hear the daughter's words over the blare of the TV. Father and daughter were comparing hands, and even from a distance Stella saw the similarity, since not many fifteen-year-old girls have such stubby peasant hands. Jack, however, seemed unmoved, and after half an hour or so, during which the boyfriend was admitted from the cold for a brief audience, Gabrielle, who had been napping on the daybed despite all the racket, began to stir. Something in the girl's voice roused her, and she mistook it for the voice of her own dear, departed daughter. Bewildered by her own longing, the old woman called out querulously, "Carolyn?" Then she apparently recognized her mistake, as well as the identity of the granddaughter she had denied having for fifteen years, and demanded that Jan leave the house. Stella took the cue, announcing that Jan and John were upsetting her mother-in-law and they would have to leave. A couple phrases passed between the father and daughter, but again Stella failed to catch them, and soon the young couple vanished into the outside world from which they had mysteriously appeared.

Finally, during their second winter in Lowell, Jack tired of his mother's complaints about the cold and acceded to her wish to move south. He found a house just around the corner from the one where they had first lived in St. Petersburg, put the Sanders Avenue property on the market, and prepared to abandon his hometown for the last time. To make more cash to finance the move, Jack had written some magazine articles and signed a contract for yet another novel, to be called *Vanity of Duluoz*, which he dedicated to Stella, using her Greek name, Stavroula, and playing upon its meaning, "from the cross." It seems that he was aware not only of the suffering he felt, but also of the suffering he caused. In the spring of 1967 Stella found herself in a station wagon owned by one of Jack's Lowell buddies, bound for the first time for a home away from Lowell.

If Gabrielle's condition was eased by the move, Jack's was made worse. He found both old and new friends with whom to carouse, and his depression deepened when he discovered that the house he had just purchased had come with a hidden tax lien. Suddenly, he learned that he must pay almost two thousand dollars in back taxes or lose the house to the state. Beside himself, he called his agent in New York to beg for a loan, and when Sterling Lord refused, Jack, in tears, handed the phone to Stella. From that point, she took charge. If the Lord would not provide, the Sampas family would. Stella borrowed the money from one of her brothers, then immediately began to take in sewing to earn the money to pay back the loan. Jack, even in the face of seeing his family thrown out of their home, seemed incapable of doing any work except writing. Fortunately for him and his mother, Stella was not so picky.

And still she fought the battle against alcoholism. Gabrielle kept a little bell by her bedside, so she could ring if she needed help. When Jack's nephew, Paul Blake Jr., visited, he found Jack sitting in a rocking chair in the middle of the living room floor, swigging from a bottle of scotch and watching TV, while his grandmother rang from her bedroom, demanding that Stella light her a cigarette and pour her a glass of brandy, which she kept in a bureau drawer. In his drunken paranoia Jack had apparently begun divorce proceedings against Stella — who knows how he thought he would take care of himself and his mother without her? — and sometimes Gabrielle taunted her daughter-in-law with the threat of divorce.

In the face of these conditions, Stella changed her strategy in dealing with Jack's drinking buddies. Instead of trying to keep them away, she now invited them to drink in her house, reasoning that at least that way she wouldn't have to worry what was happening to Jack in the bars, or pay his fines after he got thrown in jail. This tactic also discouraged Jack's less reputable companions from coming around. Jack continued his late-night phone sessions, however, even going so far as to invite Edie Parker to visit them on the pretext that it would be good for Gabrielle to see her and to discuss the old days. Stella, of course, objected strenuously.

Under these circumstances Jack somehow managed to finish his novel, in many ways a revision of his first published book, and *Vanity of Duluoz* became the last novel to appear during his lifetime. Still sorely in need of cash, he cast around for a new subject, and instead came up with an old one. He began revising a long outtake from *On the Road*, a story about the family troubles of a young black boy in North Carolina. This novella, published posthumously as *Pic*, was virtually the only story Jack ever told in the third person. But Jack continued to squander money as fast as he made it. *Vanity of Duluoz*, despite its artful retelling of Jack's transition from late adolescence to young manhood, was received coolly by the public and the critics. Jack made a fiasco of his appearance on William F. Buckley's television talk show, *Firing Line*, which Gabrielle had originally encouraged him to accept because she liked to see her boy on national TV. Then some of Jack's friends invited him to go on an expensive European vacation. Leaving Stella to care for Gabrielle and work off the loan on the house, he squandered $2,000 in a week, including ten dollars an hour he paid a Spanish prostitute to stare into his eyes. His buddies, who assumed he would provide them with amusement, were so disgusted by his behavior that they abandoned him. Jack wended his drunken way back to Florida alone.

By September 1969 most of Jack's old friends were refusing to accept his late-night phone calls. Even Carolyn Cassady had cut

Jack off following Neal's death in February 1968. Yet Jack still wrote to Edie, insisting that she would be welcome to visit them, but offering to come to Detroit if she couldn't come to Florida. He reached out to his past as to a life raft. There is some indication that he began to reach out to Stella, as well. After a serious bar brawl in a predominantly black Tampa nightclub, Jack was jailed. He had been beaten so badly that he required stitches, and once again Stella had to spend money they didn't have to bail him out. Still Jack continued to consume massive amounts of whiskey, but back home, with his face beaten black and blue, he was sometimes now moved to declare his love for Stella and to recognize how much he owed to her for keeping together what little remained of his social life.

In the third week of October 1969, Jack, who despite his self-abuse had remained surprisingly healthy, began to vomit blood. Stella became alarmed when he complained how much his stomach hurt, something he had never done before. On the nineteenth she was forced to call an ambulance and see her husband admitted to the hospital. Despite continued blood transfusions over the next thirty-six hours, Jack died of internal hemorrhage on October 21. Stella made the arrangements to take him home for the last time, and Jack's funeral was held in the big St. Jean Baptiste church on Moody Street in Lowell. He was buried in the Sampas family plot in Edson Cemetery, just a few paces from Stella's brother, Sebastian, Jack's boyhood friend. In death, Jack officially became a member of the Sampas clan.

At the visitation in Archambault Funeral Home, Stella was shielded from an outrageous bit of effrontery when one of her brothers spotted two well-dressed women enter the parlor where Jack was laid out in a hideous hound's-tooth jacket and red bow tie. Approaching the women, he asked politely who they were. The older one, a buxom blonde in her late forties, announced loudly, "I'm Mrs. Jack Kerouac." It was, of course, Edie Parker. Eventually that week in Lowell, Stella met and even befriended Edie, as did her brother Tony. In the following months both of them wrote kind letters to her, encouraging Edie to write her memoirs and publish Jack's letters to her, and in Tony's case, advising her how to deal with Ann Charters, who had already begun work on her landmark biography of Jack. Edie had learned from Jack's literary friends at the funeral just how important a writer he might become after his death, and fresh out of her third marriage, she was already at pains to re-enter her first, if posthumously, as it were.

Back in Florida with Gabrielle, who was still wailing over the loss of her "little boy," Stella got another shock when she read Jack's will. To her surprise, he had left everything to his mother, not even mentioning her name in the document. The alternate heir, in the event that Gabrielle should have died before Jack, was Paul Blake Jr., who was now serving in the air force, stationed in Texas. As executor, Jack had appointed a local bank. Fortunately for Stella, as she discovered, Florida law includes a provision known by the antique term dowry rights, which guarantees the widow at least one third of her spouse's estate, regardless of the expressed provisions of his will. Not that Stella foresaw any trouble from Gabrielle, who was now almost completely dependent on her daughter-in-law, but in legal matters, Stella knew, one must be cautious. As executor, the bank naturally exercised such caution. Learning of the existence of Jack's daughter, they dispatched a court official to find her in New Mexico and offered her a nominal sum to renounce any future claim on her father's house. That was just about all there was of his estate in 1969, and Stella was particularly worried about the house, which she herself had worked hard to save from the tax lien and which would now provide her only personal security as she turned to the care of Gabrielle.

I'm not sure what thought was given to Paul Blake Jr., but in any event he was preoccupied with his military duties, which soon took him to Vietnam, where the conflict was nearing the height of its intensity. Paul's main concern was over the loss of his Uncle Jack, who had served as his surrogate father both before and after his parents' divorce. Soon Paul got himself into trouble with the military authorities for refueling jets without proper authorization, and he spent the next few years first negotiating, with the help of his father, a transfer into the army, then finishing out his tour of duty in combat. When he finally got back to Florida, his grandmother was also dead, and Paul discovered that many of his high school friends believed he had been killed in action. However the rumor got started, he assumed that Gabrielle and Stella had heard it too, and that his grandmother died believing that she was the last of her immediate family. At least that was how he explained to himself Stella's apparent shock when he appeared on her doorstep the year after Gabrielle's death with his own young son in tow, looking for a handout.

In fact, during the next decade Stella tried hard to keep in touch with Paul. He was, after all, a member of her family. She often sent him small gifts of money enclosed in her Christmas cards, and once she loaned him $500 to help him get on his feet. But in the years immediately following Jack's death she had her hands full. For a while she and Gabrielle thought about returning to Massachusetts, where they would be near their families in case they needed help. Stella herself wasn't exactly young anymore. In advance of their possible move, she shipped Jack's literary archive back to Lowell, and it found a home in an upstairs room of the Sampas family home. If there ever was any hope of doing a professional scholarly evaluation of Kerouac's organization of his own archives, it was lost during the years immediately following his death. Of course, if the Sampases had been a different kind of people, they might have trashed the stuff instead of saving it. On the other hand, if Kerouac, who was at the nadir of his reputation as an author in the late 1960s, had shown more promise of lasting literary greatness, they might have immediately hired a scholar to help them place the material in a research library, where it would have been carefully catalogued. As it was, Jack's papers, like his reputation, went into limbo for two decades.

In 1973 the first published biography, Ann Charters' *Kerouac*, appeared. In an account published in *Kerouac's Town*, Barry Gifford catalogued some of Stella's objections to Charters' version of Jack's life, not the least of which was the report that Carolyn Kerouac had committed suicide, a mistake that deeply offended both Stella's and Gabrielle's religious beliefs. Given her upbringing, and apparently oblivious of the so-called sexual revolution, Stella was also understandably shocked and offended by the amount of attention Charters paid to Jack's sex life. Of course, from the distance of the late 1990s, I think it's also safe to say that these details might have irritated Stella's memory of her own sex life with Jack. Nevertheless, *Kerouac* became a cult classic that has never been out of print since it first appeared. Charters has her own talent for storytelling, which she later demonstrated in her editing of Kerouac's *Selected Letters*, and her biography reads more like a novel than a documentary. If any single work or person is responsible for the high value now placed on Jack's estate, it is probably *Kerouac* and Charters.

Stella, however, failed to appreciate the great service such a biography might do for her own net worth. Her sensitivity to a single issue overrode her interest in helping to build her late husband's literary reputation, and from 1973 until her death, whenever anyone asked about her relationship with Jack, she gave a standard reply: "If you want to know about Jack's life, read his books." Not bad advice, really, just a narrow view of the possibilities. As a result of this narrowness — which as I say is entirely understandable — Kerouac's reputation continued to be sustained and passed on largely by word of mouth, while his academic reputation was frozen by the blast of negative criticism leveled at him in the late 1950s. Though she did consent to sign a contract with Aaron Latham, the screenwriter responsible for *Urban Cowboy*, Latham failed to produce the "authorized" biography within the allotted five years, and so defaulted. For her own good reasons and perfectly within her rights, Stella subsequently denied biographers and scholars access to the kind of materials they need to conduct their research: letters, notebooks, and such.

At some point in the early 1970s, according to Paul Blake Jr., he and his father tried to get Stella to allow Gabrielle to come live with them and, according to John Sampas, to take charge of Jack's archives, but Stella refused, probably for both practical and sentimental reasons. Gabrielle, for her part, seems to have been quite content under her daughter-in-law's care, and as late as 1972 she was writing to her relatives to express her continued satisfaction with the arrangement. Then in October 1973 Gabrielle died. This time Stella was not only named in a Kerouac will, but named sole heir and executrix. It is this will, dated February 13, 1973, and filed officially on November 15, 1973, that ultimately became the bone of contention in Jan Kerouac's lawsuit to gain a share of the estate.

In a phone conversation in 1995 Rod Anstee, a Canadian Kerouac collector, told me that he was probably the person who tipped Gerry Nicosia to the fact that both witnesses to Gabrielle's will lived at the same address, which happened to be next door to the Kerouac house in St. Petersburg. As it turned out, the signatures were those of a gay couple, one of whom was Gabrielle's physical therapist. The will was apparently drawn up at the lawyer's office, then sent home to Gabrielle for her signature. Whether she actually signed in the presence of the witnesses became an issue in the lawsuit. Someone also observed that Gabrielle's signature was somewhat irregular, and that her last name appears to be misspelled. I am looking at a copy of her will as I write this, and there does appear to be an extra loop after the r and before the o in Kerouac. Since I am not a handwriting expert, I can't judge the authenticity of the signature. But Gabrielle was old and feeble, as well as partially paralyzed, so an extra loop, even in her own signature, wouldn't have been unexpected, and other documents she signed in the last years before her death show the identical irregularity. Besides, as I have already said, to believe the will was forged, you would have to attribute actions to Stella that seem completely out of character, and that is something I am not prepared to do.

At any rate, after exactly seven years of loving servitude to her husband and his mother, Stella was back on her own. After deciding to keep the Florida house to be used as a family vacation home, she moved back to Lowell, where she resumed life as she had known it until Jack intervened in 1966. Biographers Dennis McNally, Gerry Nicosia, Charles Jarvis (though himself a Lowell Greek), and Tom Clark were turned away. As far as I know, besides her talk with Barry Gifford, Stella gave only one interview, and that was to Jack's friend and former physician, Dr. Danny DeSole.

In the 1980s, however, members of Jack Kerouac's extended family began to intersect with Stella again. In 1982 Stella denied Joyce Johnson permission to quote from Jack's letters to Joyce in her memoir, the moving account of her youth and her year-and-a-half relationship with Jack, Minor Characters. A year or two later,

Stella received word that Jan's lawyer in Santa Fe had contacted Sterling Lord, claiming that his client was owed back royalties on all her father's books. After more than a year of negotiations, Jan settled with Stella for about $5,000 (in Jan's recollection it was $7,000), with the understanding that in the future they would share all domestic royalties fifty-fifty. Stella seems to have acted her part in this in good faith, and Jan apparently felt no bitterness toward her at the time. But then the true weirdness started to come down.

Against his advice and better judgment, Jim Perrizo, who had been acting as Edie Parker's secretary, wrote to the Lord Agency stating Edie's intention to claim the royalties of On the Road as belonging to her alone, on the grounds that her marriage with Jack had never been legally dissolved and that she was unmarried at the time of his death, both demonstrably false assertions. Edie neglected to mention either the annulment of her first marriage or her two subsequent marriages. Jim and others who knew Edie are still baffled about her motives for adopting this hostile attitude toward Stella, who had always been friendly to Edie. My guess is it involved a kind of hubris, the same overweening pride that impelled Edie to insist on her own version of the past in the face of contradictory evidence. It took months for Stella and Sterling Lord to straighten out this mess with the Library of Congress, where copyrights and renewals are recorded, especially in light of the recent addition of Jan's name to all the paperwork.

But Edie didn't stop there. With the help of a friend who worked in one of the Detroit-area offices of the Social Security Administration, she proceeded to file a claim to receive Jack's death benefits, again using the argument that Jack and Edie had never been legally divorced. Stella's Florida lawyer, Stephen Stein, was forced to track down a copy of Jack and Edie's annulment from 1946, which Edie perhaps assumed had been destroyed by a fire in the Wayne County clerk's office in later years. It's a wonder Edie wasn't arrested for fraud. But now Stella was on her guard, and while she was searching through her own records she came up with a copy of Joan Haverty's Mexican divorce from Kerouac in 1957, which Stella had procured before her own marriage to Jack in 1966.

As it happened, Joan let her interests be served vicariously through Jan. Aside from the vivid stories she told to her neighbors on Bell Avenue about her brief life with Kerouac and her other youthful adventures in New York, Joan seemed to focus on the present. Just before she left Ellensburg to be near the twins in Eugene, however, she reconnected with Herb Lashinsky, her old boyfriend from thirty years ago, the man she'd been entertaining in her loft the night she first met Kerouac. According to Jan, her mother was already menopausal, and she renewed her relationship with Herb as a kind of last fling. Then just as suddenly as he had reappeared, Herb disappeared — this time for good. Joan got a simple phone call informing her that her old lover was dead.

About this time Joan also began to reinvent herself. This was partly a result of the fantasies she shared with her son about moving to Scotland. She had always been proud of her mother's family history, though she tended to look askance at her father's Irish heritage. In high school Joan's fascination with her selective ethnicity earned her the nickname Scotty, and in the late 1970s she changed her name unofficially to Stuart. As Joan V. Stuart, she also became interested in grass-roots politics, and before she left Ellensburg she began to do volunteer work for the local community action organization. At the same time, while she lived in the upstairs of the big red house on Ruby Street, she returned probably the only city directory information form she ever filled out in her life. On it she listed her occupation as "free lance writer," although I have yet to discover anything she ever published besides the 1961 article in Confidential (which is, by the way, well-written — if not, as Nicosia claims, ghostwritten).

By the time she and David moved down to Oregon, then, Joan was primed to begin a new life. After she got her household established in west Eugene, she applied to become a VISTA volunteer, was accepted, and at the ripe old age of 50, despite the onset of breast cancer, this inveterate outsider became an activist. She devoted most of her energy to improving conditions in her own neighborhood. Her attempt to reserve an open field at the west end of Bell Avenue for a neighborhood park became the symbol of her struggle. Largely because her neighbors both liked and trusted her and partly because of her dignified middle-class bearing and articulate language, she succeeded. When I visited her old neighborhood in the summer of 1995, Trainsong Park, for which Jan named her second novel, was filled with playground equipment, happy children, and gossiping parents. Perhaps because of the park, the neighborhood has remained fairly stable, and one of the neighbors graciously led me to an apple tree Joan had asked him to transplant from her yard into the park just a month or so before her death. Joan's activism also attracted the attention of the local lesbian community, and Jan recalled that a large number of gay women attended Joan's funeral in 1990. For the most part, even at the end, she led a quiet, independent life, intelligently following her own desires and bending the system to her own needs, rather than bending herself to its.

Stella herself, after warding off Edie's bizarre attempts to supplant her as Kerouac's lawful widow, barely survived the dedication of the memorial to Jack in Lowell in June 1988. In the last few years of her life she became a caregiver again, when her aged mother was no longer able to care for herself. Stella died in St. Joseph's Hospital in Lowell on February 10, 1990, just three months before Joan, whom she had never met. She spent much of her life caring for others, and in the end she was rewarded by the universal admiration of all those who were close to her, both family and friends. Only outsiders have criticized her for closing the Kerouac archive, and that, to me, seems a small matter compared to love and respect. And besides, fans, biographers, scholars, and critics aren't family.

Edie outlived her comrades in Kerouac wifedom by a mere three years, and when she died, she left behind a bit of controversy over her own estate, which included a number of valuable Kerouac artifacts, including the letters he had written her over the years. All these things went to a fellow named Tim Moran, who had succeeded Jim Perrizo as Edie's secretary. When Charlotte Pattison, Edie's sister, contested the deathbed will, however, Jim was subpoenaed to testify. Based on Jim's long service to Edie and thorough knowledge of Beat literature, the probate judge expressed the private belief that Jim should have inherited Edie's papers, but unable to find fault with the will, he upheld it, and

Lawrence Ferlinghetti, Allen Ginsberg, and Stella Sampas Kerouac at
the dedication of the Kerouac Memorial, Lowell, MA, October 1988

Tim Moran now legally owns Edie's Kerouac memorabilia, valued, incidentally, at about $17,000.

In my mind the controversy over Stella Sampas's — i.e., Jack
Kerouac's — estate resulted partly from our inability to distinguish the legal, ethical, and moral aspects of the case. Being a
pragmatist, I'll take them in reverse order. Morally, there are two
questions. Did Jack's neglect of his daughter entitle her to a share
of his estate, regardless of the legalities? Most people, without
much hesitation, will say yes. Even John Sampas, if you had asked
him in 1991, was willing to give her, if not a third, at least some
share of the estate. After the lawsuit, of course, he wouldn't have
even spoken to her if she had asked. One does not file lawsuits
against members of one's own family in Lowell — at least not

without repercussions. Based on my own experience, something in Jan's personality inclined her more toward divisiveness than reconciliation. I believe she thrived on the dramatic aspects of the lawsuit, and like her mother, her own independence made the moral issue virtually irrelevant to her. Still, I would side with the majority, who seem to feel that Jan was deprived morally, if not legally or otherwise, of her rightful share in her father's estate.

The second moral question concerns Paul Blake Jr., who is far less aggressive than Jan was, but who stands in a very similar position to Jan's, at least in relation to their grandmother, if not to Jack. While the blood tie of uncle and nephew is not as close as that of father and daughter, of all people now living, Paul Blake Jr. has the most intimate knowledge of Jack over the last two decades of his life. Paul grew up with his uncle, and as I have mentioned, Jack did name Paul in his will, in case anything happened to Gabrielle. That brings me to the next point. With regard to Gabrielle, whose will lay at the heart of Jan's lawsuit, Jan and Paul stand in the same relation as grandchildren. That's why he was named as a respondent rather than as a co-petitioner in Jan's lawsuit. It's every person for herself in the legal realm. Why didn't Gabrielle, who doted upon Paul, provide for him in her will? Does he have a moral right to a share of his uncle's estate because of the love he bore for Jack's mother, Paul's grand-mother? The same people — that is, a majority of those asked to consider the issue — who take Jan's side in the first question would probably take Paul's side in the second by analogy. Again, I side with the majority. Jack once painted a portrait of Paul, and he promised him he could have the baseball game Jack made up when he was a child and played most of his life (though Nicosia says it was lost in the 1960s). Morally, I believe that's the least Paul Blake Jr. deserves.

If the lawsuit accomplished nothing else, it put Jan and Paul in touch. Once when I called Jan in February 1995 she announced ecstatically that her lawyer had finally tracked Paul down. After leaving his last job in Alaska he had dropped out of sight for sixteen months. Unemployed, homeless, alcoholic, estranged from his second wife, he had been driving around the West, living in his van. When he finally settled again in rural Sacramento, where I visited him in August 1995, his life began to stabilize. To her credit, Jan saw past the legal implications of their relationship, and for the remainder of her life, the next fifteen months, she treated Paul like a long-lost cousin, if not a brother. As I said before, a lot of this business has to do with Jan's desire to create a family for herself.

Now the ethical issue: Should Jack Kerouac's archive be consolidated in one location for the benefit of scholars? Frankly, as a sometime scholar myself, I can't see that it makes much difference. First of all, Kerouac material is already spread out among several locations, including such distantly separated places as the New York Public Library and the Ransom Humanities Center at the University of Texas–Austin. Scholars are used to this sort of thing, and I for one enjoy traveling to different venues to do research. Of course, when these libraries digitize their holdings and put them on-line, this question will become moot.

Gerry Nicosia's main complaint is that some unpublished materials are being sold off to collectors by John Sampas. This could be a problem, because these collectors (keep in mind that there has long been a market for Kerouaciana, and this business picks up as his estate grows more valuable), don't have any responsibility to share their purchases with the public. In addition, collectors have to sell things to make a profit, and one easy way to make a profit is to buy some Kerouac artifacts in a lot, then sell them off piecemeal. One sale that gained an undue amount of publicity was Johnny Depp's purchase of Kerouac's raincoat for a reported $15,000. Now while it's conceivable that Kerouac's wardrobe might become an object of research for future scholars of the history of costume, that seems unlikely. The estate presumably exists to provide its heirs with income, and articles of clothing would appear to be the most dispensable part of Kerouac's belongings. John Sampas admits that he made some mistakes early on in his administration of the estate, thanks mostly to bad advice. So would you or I, in all likelihood, since most of us lack knowledge of how literary estates should be handled. John now assures the public that "ninety percent" of Kerouac's papers are going to the New York Public Library, where some of them are already on deposit, if not bought and paid for, thanks to the high value now placed on Kerouac materials.

Another point. Others besides John have sold off Kerouac materials. Paul Blake Jr., for instance, hard up in the 1980s, sold his collection to the New York Public Library, which is how the last letter Jack ever wrote came to reside in the Berg Collection there. Even Jan and Gerry, in the midst of their crusade to publicize their version of the lawsuit, sold an old arrest warrant relating to Joan's paternity suit against Jack in the late 1950s to finance a fund-raising event. Ironically, one of John Sampas's agents spotted the warrant at a book fair in Boston, and John purchased it for his own collection. Edie bequeathed her Kerouac papers to Tim Moran. I suppose you *could* put nebulous considerations about keeping Kerouac's archives together before self-interest, but I don't think you should be expected to, especially if you have to put bread on the table. Besides, the selective sale of Kerouac materials — for example, Johnny Depp's old raincoat — serves marketing purposes that ultimately increase the value of the rest. In the few years he has administered the estate, John Sampas has learned a great deal about the marketing of his collection.

Parenthetically, let me add a practical consideration. So far as I know, no one in the media asked the obvious question: What would happen to Kerouac's archive if Gerry Nicosia pursues and wins Jan's lawsuit? The answer is, since her heirs stand to gain at most a two-thirds share of her father's estate, that the chances of the archive's being further fragmented would be even greater in this event than they are under the present circumstances. Perhaps Gerry Nicosia and John Sampas could reconcile their differences and agree on how to dispose of Kerouac's papers — there is a prophecy in which the lion lies down with the lamb. Actually, I can see only endless complications that might prevent scholars from gaining access to these materials for decades if Jan's suit succeeds. Which brings me to the legal issue.

For someone trying to unravel all the issues involved in Jack Kerouac's legacy, the worst thing about the lawsuit is the rhetoric it generated. Gerry Nicosia, who has a mind like a steel trap for facts, bends his wealth of knowledge to suit a kind of conspiracy theory. In his view everything that happened was intended (by

John Sampas or his henchmen) as an attack on Jan or as a personal slight against Gerry. Naturally, in typical Lowell fashion, John takes offense at such accusations. At the 1995 NYU Kerouac conference, for instance, I was sitting with John on the balcony of the student union overlooking Washington Square. I showed him a pointedly partisan poem in the form of an anagram of the word SAMPAS, self-published by one of Jan's most visible supporters. John thought one of the lines questioned Stella's virtue, and before I knew it he was in the poet's face, threatening to punch his lights out if he didn't offer the family an apology and print a retraction. Such confrontations are to be expected in the polarized atmosphere surrounding the lawsuit, but predictable as they are, they don't do Jack Kerouac much good. There are still lots of academics with 1950s prejudices whose only association with his writing is his disreputable behavior. Besides rousing emotions, rhetoric serves only to limit the perspective of the discussion. In Gerry's hands, it has also blurred the distinction I am trying to make here between the moral, the ethical, and the legal.

Legally, John Sampas administers the estate of his late sister, Stella, who left her brothers and sisters her share in various Kerouac books. She made her bequests quite specific, rather than putting her money into one big pot. John, for instance, personally inherited Stella's interest in all Jack's unpublished writing, presumably a treasure trove, since the royalties from publication of these would not have to be shared with anyone. Another brother received Stella's share of the royalties from *On the Road*, a sizable sum, since Jan told me that it accounted for about half of her annual income. And so on. To simplify this complicated business, the Sampas family elected John, the youngest brother, who was self-employed at the time Stella died, to oversee and coordinate the business of her estate, and to my mind he has done a credible job.

As for Jan's status, remember two facts. First, in 1961 a New York court determined that she was, indeed, the daughter of Jack Kerouac, and after that time he assumed the minimal responsibility of providing some monetary support for her until she married John Lash. Thus, since 1961 there has never been any legal question about Jan's paternity. Second, in the early 1970s Jan signed away her rights to her father's house for a nominal sum. Whether this can be construed to mean that she gave up all interest in his estate, or whether it was a fully informed decision on her part, remains to be seen. Certainly, it was an inadvisable decision, given the outcome. Nevertheless, she did sign the papers.

To tell the truth, I delayed the conclusion of this book, hoping that the lawsuit would be settled and I could hang my last words on a final legal decision. Then Jan died, and the issue became even more complicated, since her two heirs, with Gerry Nicosia as her literary executor, had to decide whether to continue the suit or drop it. Then John Sampas informed me in December 1996 that Jan's heirs were planning to drop the lawsuit, but that Gerry Nicosia was attempting to pursue it on his own, if matters weren't confusing enough already. (If you've followed me this far, I suppose it wasn't too confusing.) In September 1998, the New Mexico Appellate Court denied Gerry's request to be allowed to pursue the lawsuit as Jan's literary executor, and the Bernalillo County Probate Court declared Jan's estate officially closed. Though this latter decision technically ends Gerry's tenure as literary executor, he has appealed it to the New Mexico Supreme Court. And more potential confusion lies down the road, in the person of Judy Machado, a Lowellite who has hired an attorney to represent her claim that she is the illegitimate daughter of Jack Kerouac and Mary Carney, his old high school flame.

But *Use My Name* isn't really about lawsuits or legal issues. At heart it's about families, and the children and women and men who form them. In that sense it sheds an entirely new light on the meaning of the political buzzword of our day: family values. A conservative reader might be moved to say, "Well, if more of these people had practiced strong family values, much pain would have been prevented." Perhaps. But the thing that makes this story remarkable is that it's not remarkable at all. Only Jack Kerouac's writing is remarkable. Or Stella Sampas's devotion. Or Joan Stuart's independence. Or Jan Kerouac's spirit of adventure. But the kind of family — both physical and legal and spiritual — they created by their interactions is as old as Western culture and as new as a postmodern sitcom. For that reason I found it worth investigating and writing about.

But I chose to tell the story of these people in the way I have told it because I too am an heir of the legacy of Jack Kerouac. In my case that means that in the face of all his flaws and foibles, his meanness and his sins, I remain devoted to the spirit of his writing, a spirit I wish to see flourish and grow in America in the coming century. Each one of the participants in this broadly extended family affair had a life as profound and meaningful as Jack Kerouac's, yet theirs have been viewed only in the light of his, in his own novels and in the later biographies of him. Here, I wanted simply to present their stories in their own light and to show, at the risk of repeating the description of some events as many as five times, incidentally, how Jack Kerouac, road novelist and American pop hero, might have looked from the points of view of five people to whom he was intimately related.

ELEVEN

AUTO/BIOGRAPHY: WAR STORIES OR PARASITOLOGY?

The first time I ever talked to Jan Kerouac on the phone, in January 1995, she told me she had just signed a contract for Francis Ford Coppola's film version of her father's most famous novel, *On the Road*. She was to get $10,000 to act as "creative advisor." Several weeks later *Newsweek* carried a story about the first casting call for the movie. Flyers had gone up in the New York City area explaining that the protocol would require actors to read a selection of their choice from one of Jack's novels. Within hours all the bookstores in Manhattan had sold out of *On the Road*, despite the difficulty clerks noted in their customers' ability to pronounce the novelist's last name. Jan's response to the whole episode was gleeful: "Oh boy, that means pretty soon I'll get a big check from Viking" (the publisher of *On the Road*). I don't know if the check ever came, because two months after our first conversation, Jan "fired" me as her biographer.

I put fired in quotation marks because I was never hired in the first place. I got the idea to do the biography while I was living in Ireland in the autumn of 1994. I had been wanting to write a biography for several years, but the proper subject never presented itself. For a while, I considered Neal Cassady, the model for the character Dean Moriarty in *On the Road* and for that of Cody Pomeray in several of Jack's other books. But the thought of having to hang out with the people Cassady hung out with later in his life daunted me. Then I discovered that a New York artist named Kim Spurlock had already done a significant amount of research into Cassady's Denver years, as had Tom Christopher, who published collections of documents relating to Cassady's life in 1995 and 1998, and I was relieved that somebody else was busy filling in the gap in the record left by William Plummer's biography, *The Holy Goof*.

In September 1994 I went with the poet Brett Eugene Ralph to speak at the Lowell Celebrates Kerouac! festival, an annual event organized by local Kerouac experts and fans. There, for the first time, I actually came face-to-face with Jan Kerouac. I had seen her read twice before, once at the Beats Conference sponsored by New York University the previous spring. In Greenwich Village that May of 1994 she had seemed muddled. Like many other spectators, I assumed she was drunk or spaced out on drugs. In the middle of a silly rap song about her genius father, she forgot the words and had to apologize to the band for screwing up. But hey, that's standard behavior for writers whose pantheon includes such notorious bad boys as Gregory Corso. Or so I thought at the time. In Lowell, Jan and her aide-de-camp, Gerry Nicosia, were flushed with the initial success of their lawsuit against the Kerouac estate. In May, shortly after the NYU lolla-palooza, a probate judge in Pinellas County, Florida, reopened his estate after more than twenty years. The smell of money filled the air like gun smoke, and John Sampas, I soon learned, was "the enemy." For Jan Kerouac — and perhaps for Gerry Nicosia as well — winning the war over Jack's estate had already become a raison d'être. And believe me, with as much as $10 million at stake in Jack's estate by some estimates, it was an all-out war, no holds barred, thermonuclear weapons notwithstanding.

At a public forum on the Washington Square campus of NYU I had watched fascinated from my perch in an empty balcony as Gerry, speaking from the podium, confronted John Sampas, sitting in the audience near the press section, about the "destruc-tion" of the Kerouac archive. Sampas, exercising his current legal rights, had been selling off some articles of Kerouac's cloth-ing to people with big enough money to buy such mementos. Nicosia waxed righteous, his voice strident with indignation. The Kerouac estate must be kept intact, he argued, sold to a single large university library rather than parceled out to unscrupulous collectors — war profiteers — to be lost to scholars forever.

I wondered, perhaps perversely, if Gerry had a stake in a unified sale beyond the fact that the Bancroft Library at Berkeley, which is not too far from where he lives, had been a bidder for the Kerouac collection. Rumors were rife that spring in New York, and high among them ranked the hearsay that Sampas had turned down first $1 million, then $2 million, for Jack's once meticulously organized personal archive. No one seemed to know whether the second sum included payment for the legendary scroll manuscript of On the Road, itself appraised at $1 million.

Sampas defended himself manfully, asserting his legal right to do whatever he pleased as the appointed administrator of his sister's estate. While Allen Ginsberg sat nearby with a pained look on his usually serene Buddhist countenance, John yelled up toward the podium that Gerry had no right whatever even to comment on the disposition of matters in which he had no legal standing, especially to the extent of contacting the New York Public Library to see which of Jack's notebooks John had already sold or given to their collection. Gerry, for his part, shot back a truism: we live in a free country, he said, and he, Gerry Nicosia, could — and would — speak with whomever he pleased. The acrid air in the hall crackled with tension until the moderator called the session to a hasty close.

Four months later in Lowell, Ginsberg told a local newspaper reporter that he was too old for such wrangling. I guess he just wanted to enjoy the splendor of his declining years as the greatest American poet of the second half of this century. Of course, Buddhists have always espoused nonviolence, and then, too, Ginsberg himself had just recently sold his own extensive archive — including a pair of his underwear and clippings from his 1960s beard — to Stanford University for a reported $2 million. After nearly five decades of assiduous yet delighted labor in the fields of poetry and social activism, he deserved a quiet retirement. And Ginsberg, more than any other single individual, was primarily responsible for keeping Jack Kerouac's name in lights on the crowded postmodern marquee. In fact, he tried valiantly to stage-manage the NYU conference in 1994, as well as a similar one held the following year solely to honor Jack's literary achievement.

It occurred to me as I watched John Sampas and Gerry Nicosia exchange verbal salvos that their animosity more closely resembled the savage and chaotic competition of parasites than the tactics of a pitched battle. As a practiced parasite myself (dignified by the term journalist, scholar, or writer), I readily recognize my own kind. It has several species, some of which have to work harder than others to get a square meal. There are freelance parasites like Gerry, whose families usually support to some extent their own often thankless industry. There are subsidized parasites like me, who earn a living primarily from teaching (which is far from easy if you do it right) and use our research as an excuse to feed off the creativity of others and to nose into the lives of artists and the people they associate with, although their subjects have usually been dead for decades, if not centuries. Then there are parasites like Jan, who came up hard in a welfare family in Alphabet City, worked her way up from drug abuse and petty crime through menial jobs in the restaurant business to write several unspectacular autobiographical novels, and finally to lay claim to a share of an inheritance which, from my layman's point of view, she unquestionably deserves. Next, there are parasites like John Sampas, who had this ignoble status thrust upon him by his family and the law, and who by one of those amazing twists of fate has now come to control — to some extent — the destiny of the reputation of one of America's most original writers. Last but not least, there are the lawyers, including Thomas Brill, Herbert Jacoby, and Saul Cohen on Jan's side and Lettie Marques and George Tobia on John's side. But in all fairness, lawyers only join the unholy banquet when the lower orders of parasites disagree about which of them gets to eat first. Perhaps what I am talking about is not so much a battle royal as a feeding frenzy, come to think of it. And if I am brutally honest with myself, I must admit that I am at the bottom of this food chain, which in a world of vermin means being a parasite upon other parasites.

In any case, what I saw in New York in May and in Lowell in September 1994, combined with what I already knew about Jack Kerouac, which was considerable, since I had just published a book about him in 1992, percolated down through my brain as I walked the unseasonably warm and dry streets of Dublin in

October 1994. Ireland was experiencing the mildest autumn on record. One fine afternoon after a cheap late lunch at the Well-Fed Cafe and coffee and dessert at Bewley's in Temple Bar, I was walking reflectively down Dame Street toward the gate of Trinity College, headed for my flat off Merrion Square. Suddenly and unostentatiously, as I drew alongside the monumental old Bank of Ireland, where Stephen Dedalus cashed the check for his "exhibition and essay prize" in Joyce's *Portrait of the Artist as a Young Man*, it came to me: I'll write a biography of Jan Kerouac. It was perfect. My research into her father's life and writing would provide the background, and my published book would serve as my credentials when I made my proposal to Jan herself. I had gotten Gerry's address from him after his lecture in New York, and I knew that he served as Jan's agent, among his many other activities. That night I sat at my desk looking out at the ugly IES building in Lower Fitzwilliam Street and composed a handwritten letter to Gerry announcing my idea. Next day, on my way to breakfast, I put the letter in the slime-green Irish post box by the corner newsagent's and moved the whole project to the back burner, in order to focus on my immediate duties at the Jung Centre.

In late October, returning from a week in England, where I had a chance to discuss some preliminary ideas for the biography with a literate friend, I found a postcard from Gerry expressing his approval and describing Jan's life as "an area of Beat studies that other scholars have entirely overlooked." I replied with an enthusiastic proposal for the book, requesting to be given the status of authorized biographer, even asking Gerry to serve as my agent as well. By the time I left for a month in Spain on the last day of November, however, I had heard nothing more from him, and I naturally wondered if I had been too forward or demanding in my follow-up letter. All the way down the autumnal southeast coast of Ireland I analyzed and critiqued what I had written, but when the ferry for Le Havre pulled out of Rosslare harbor, I decided to put the Jan Kerouac Biography, as I called it then, on the table alongside my recent troubles at the Jung Centre. I settled in for the twenty-two-hour trip, trying to look forward to the immediate present, to my first visit to Paris, Barcelona,

Mallorca, and Madrid, rather than to the past or the distant future. It worked. By the time my train reached the Pyrenees, I was totally absorbed in the beautifully rugged landscape leading into Catalonia.

After nearly a month of sun and speaking only Spanish, drinking cafe con leche, eating bocadillos, and sleeping in cheap but immaculate habitaciones, I managed to make it from Europe to St. Louis a half-hour before the dawn of Christmas Day, despite an icy fog that had paralyzed Heathrow for twelve hours. It was clear and cold and dry as I drove home across the entire width of Missouri with my friend Tamara, who had come to pick me up in my car. It felt strange to drive again after walking everywhere for three months. Tired as I was after nearly twenty-four hours on planes and in airports, I was also wired by jet lag and the excitement of homecoming. Occasionally, when our conversation flagged, I looked out over the moonlit, rolling Mark Twain National Forest south of I-44 and wondered if I'd find a letter from Gerry waiting, as I had when I returned to Dublin a month and a half earlier. No such luck. But in the pleasure and excitement of seeing my house all decorated and of opening presents, I forgot this small disappointment and settled in to enjoy being home for the holidays.

Early in January I wrote to Gerry at his home in Corte Madera, California, again. No reply. What had happened? Had I offended him in some way? I tried to control my Catholic guilt. He was simply busy with the holidays and other pressing matters. His usual typed postcard would arrive any day. But it never did. That second postcard to Dublin was the last written communication I received from Gerry until April. Soon, however, I got sidetracked onto the mainline, as the old country song says, finishing my first novel and starting two new ones, hoping to get them well under way before my year of unpaid leave drew to a close in August, when I would resume my duties teaching American literature.

One day near the end of the first week in January 1995, to my surprise, a letter arrived not from Gerry, but from Jan Kerouac, responding enthusiastically but ambiguously to my proposal to write a biography of her, though Gerry had obviously apprised her of my intention. There was a bonus, too: enclosed in the envelope was a copy of a letter from Jan to Sterling Lord, Jack Kerouac's literary agent, recommending me to edit the revised critical edition of *On the Road*. Such an opportunity would certainly give my academic career a boost, but knowing the uncertainty created by Jan's lawsuit for any future publication of Jack's writing, I took the letter for what it was worth — a gesture of goodwill from both Jan and Gerry, who had recommended me for the editing job.

I wanted to think about my response for a few days before I composed it, so the following Friday night Tamara and I went for dinner at some friends' house. When we got home, I found a message from Jan on the machine. She said she was looking forward to working with me on any project concerning her or her father, and she left her phone number in Albuquerque. I admit to feeling a thrill on hearing Jan's voice on my answering machine, and as I tell my students whenever I happen to blush in class, just be thankful that in our jaded world a middle-aged man is still capable of feeling such feelings. When I began speaking with her regularly on the phone, often four or five hours in a week, after I had completed my initial library research, sometimes I found myself thinking, "I'm Jan Kerouac's biographer." I told Jan this when I went to visit her in Albuquerque, and she replied matter-of-factly, "Sometimes I think to myself, 'I'm Jan Kerouac.'" This present expanded biography signifies both a loss of identity and the access of a new identity for me, if not for Jan and the other people I wound up including in it. A parasite's state of mind, precisely. I am what I write about.

A few days after the phone message I wrote to Jan stating carefully what I then had in mind: a fully researched, objective biography rather than a ghostwritten autobiography. I know now that she probably never read my letter, but if she did — as she should have — she ignored the distinction I tried to make. Though I realized that sooner or later we would have to reach a clear agreement about the project we were undertaking, I figured that at the proper time the matter would present itself for resolution. But when it finally did, it was too late. After spending seven days in March 1995 in Albuquerque laying the foundations for this book, Jan and I came to an impasse. She told me the morning I left that in our last interview, taped only the night before, she had "spilled the beans," revealed things she shouldn't have revealed about her life as a prostitute. Some terrible — perhaps irrevocable — change had taken place. Jan described it as a change in my attitude, which she thought had suddenly become voyeuristic. When I protested that she had already written about her sex life in great detail in her first novel, *Baby Driver*, she hedged, saying, "Yes, but that was fiction. You have it in my own words."

Jan Kerouac signing a poster of the "Kerouac Wears Khakis" parody of the Jack Kerouac GAP ad

And I do have it. Still. On tape, duplicated, transcribed, and now reproduced as the centerpiece of this book. Perhaps someday I'll sell it to the Bancroft Library in Berkeley, which bought Jan's "archive" from Gerry early in 1998 for a reputed $20,000. Some of Jan's and Gerry's paranoia rubbed off on me for a while. But I have the tape, and periodically I listen to it again. It does describe her activities as a prostitute and her first johns, New Mexico state politicians. The curious thing is, in the interview she hardly talks about sex, shies away from the term "intercourse," and giggles like a teenager when she has to say "blow job." It's a very serious and coherent interview, and I still think it puts her in a very good light. Near the end of the tape she explains why she stopped hooking, even though she was capable of making $100 a trick, sometimes $300 total on a good night way back in 1972. She says she didn't want to blunt herself to the possibility of romantic love in the future. Sam, my photographer friend who accompanied me on that March visit, insists that in order to feel that fear, Jan would have already had to have crossed some boundary, already blunted her ability to love beyond repair.

I don't know. I've never been there. And unfortunately, I didn't know Jan before she started hooking, so I can't compare before and after pictures. And I can't even fully understand why she came to mistrust me so rapidly and so completely. Furthermore, I'll never know, now that Jan is dead. You'll have to help decide these issues. Whatever you find in my portrait of Jan, or the depictions of the three other women and one man who knew Jack Kerouac intimately, though, remember this. It's a picture of me, too. And a picture of yourself. If you find something lacking here and there — like love — make sure the lack is in them, not in me or in yourself. If I've done anything in writing their story, I've tried to do that. Tried to make sure that I'm projecting and exploiting as little as possible, no more than is absolutely necessary to conduct human business. Still, sometimes when I review my notes, or listen to the seven or eight hours of tapes I made in Albuquerque, I feel a little bit like a voyeur, a little bit like a vampire. I admitted as much to Jan in one of our last telephone conversations, after I returned from New Mexico. I imagine you felt like that too as you read my book. It's hard not to when your role is to be a parasite upon another parasite.

It seemed doubly ironic that when Jan gave me my walking papers, firing somebody she had never even hired, her anger chose these words: "I don't want to do this with you anymore. You're a voyeuristic vampire." Before I could get or give any explanation, she hung up. Hurt and bewildered as I still am by her sudden change of heart, I have to admit, though, that I know the feeling. And now, dear reader, so do you.